Energy Circus
Chai Yi Yang
See page 50

LAND ART AS CLIMATE ACTION:

Designing
the 21st Century
City Park

Land Art
Generator Initiative
Mannheim

Kaleidoscopic Dune
Muny-Roth Chev, Jason Daniel, Vatsapol Nanta
See page 56

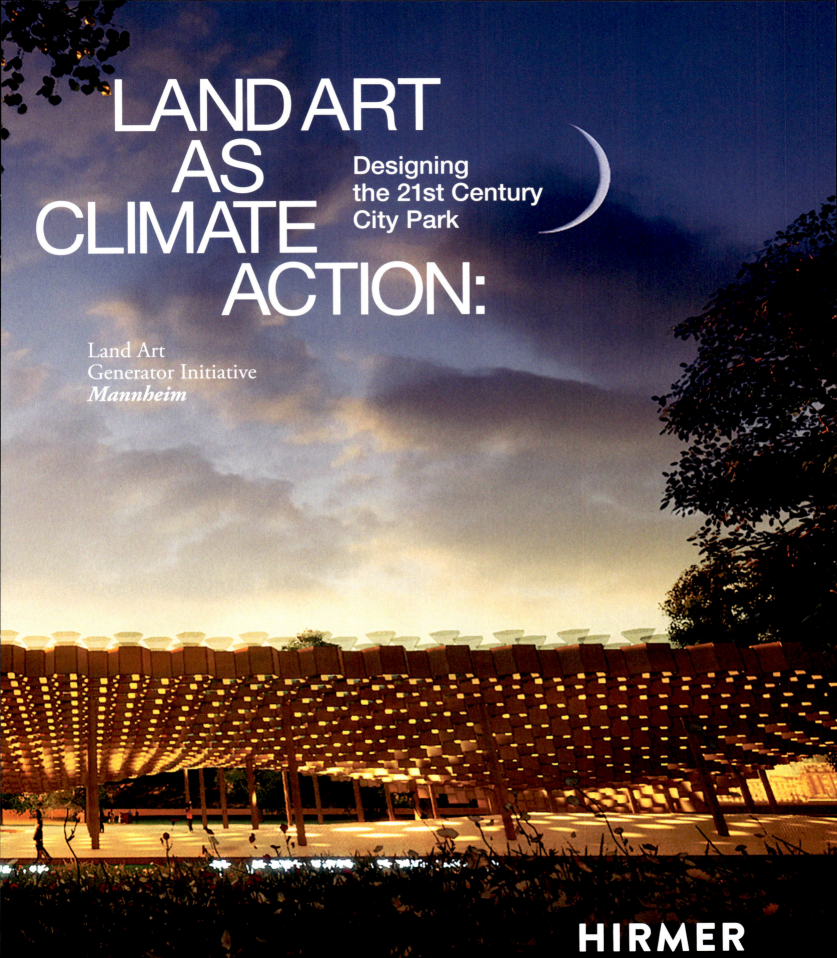

CONTENTS

8 FOREWORD
Michael Schnellbach

12 ESSAY
Designing the 21st Century City Park
Robert Ferry and Elizabeth Monoian

20 LAGI 2022 DESIGN GUIDELINES

26 ESSAY
The Becoming of Spinelli
Tina Nailor

36 ESSAY
Cultivating Photovoltaics for Producing Beauty
Alessandra Scognamiglio

40 ESSAY
Unexpected Encounters with a Garden Gnome
Sven Stremke

48 SHORTLISTED ENTRIES

174 FEATURED ENTRIES

225 BIOGRAPHIES

228 GLOSSARY

235 INDEX

236 ACKNOWLEDGMENTS

Unfold

Zicheng Zhao, Priyanjali Sinha, Andreina Sojo, Menghan Yu, Wei Xia

See page 100

Room to Breathe
Tom Esdar, Maximilian Bohnhorst, Hamed Samara
See page 198

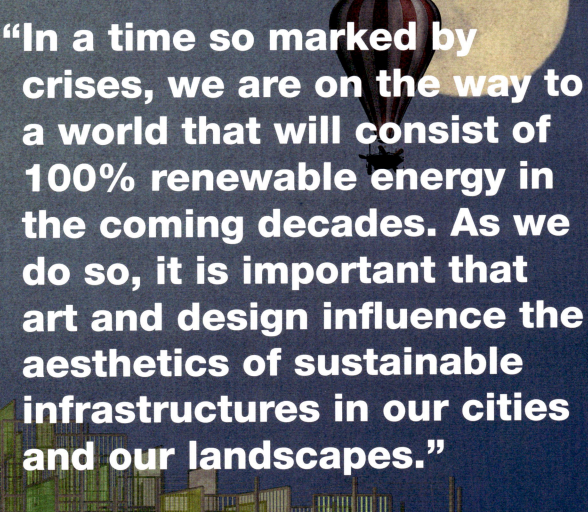

"In a time so marked by crises, we are on the way to a world that will consist of 100% renewable energy in the coming decades. As we do so, it is important that art and design influence the aesthetics of sustainable infrastructures in our cities and our landscapes."

— Michael Schnellbach
Managing Director, BUGA 23

FOREWORD

Michael Schnellbach
Managing Director
Federal Horticultural Show Mannheim 2023 /
Bundesgartenschau Mannheim 2023 gGmbH

Photograph © Daniel Lukac

Dear Reader,

The LAGI 2022 Mannheim design competition fits perfectly within the guiding themes of the Federal Horticultural Show Mannheim 2023 (BUGA 23): climate, energy, environment, and food security.

Characterizing a visionary garden show, the themes of BUGA 23 are derived from the 17 UN Sustainable Development Goals (SDGs), which BUGA 23, the City of Mannheim, and the Land Art Generator Initiative (LAGI) all embed within their visions for a sustainable future.

In a time so marked by crises, we are shifting to a world that will consist of 100% renewable energy in the coming decades. As we do so, it is important that art and design influence the aesthetics of sustainable infrastructures in our cities and our landscapes.

In our experimental field we take a playful approach to these topics of the future. This approach is also what makes the LAGI competition special.

The Land Art Generator Initiative has created a new standard for how renewable energy technologies can be integrated into our everyday lives — providing artists with the opportunity to leave a lasting cultural legacy that can serve as a reminder to future generations of this important time in history.

We are thrilled that so many creatives from around the world responded to the LAGI 2022 Mannheim design brief. Thanks to their innovation and creativity, participants in the LAGI design competition are inspiring people all over the world with the beauty and promise of a carbon neutral future and offering new ways of thinking about how we integrate sustainable infrastructure into the cultural fabric of our cities.

Just as a garden can be a productive landscape that feeds people while also providing pleasure and enjoyment, energy landscapes can combine utility and exciting design through their creation. LAGI 2022 Mannheim proves this.

It is our pleasure to collaborate with the LAGI event and exhibition within the framework of BUGA 23.

I wish you exciting insights and perhaps you too will come up with one or two creative ideas for your private space.

— Michael Schnellbach

View of the Spinelli site
Photograph © BUGA 23/Daniel Lukac

View of the Spinelli site

Photograph © BUGA 23/Daniel Lukac

ESSAY

Designing the 21st Century City Park

Robert Ferry and Elizabeth Monoian
Founding Co-Directors
Land Art Generator Initiative

Removed from a world in chaos, we take refuge in our gardens. When we place our hands into the earth we connect with the mysteries of the Universe. We ground ourselves in what really matters, with our very sustenance — with cycles of energy; the sun, wind, and water; and with the infinitely complex interrelationships between ecological systems — the nourishment that gives life to human culture.

By growing our food, maintaining our shelter, and tending to life in a garden, we enlist ourselves as Earth's stewards in a continuous struggle against entropy and disorder. As we steer through seasonal cycles, through decay and rebirth, we connect with an elusive simplicity — feelings of renewal and hope that we will try to remember when we are once again confronted with the chaos outside the garden walls.

The tradition of the German Schrebergarten or kleingarten (little garden) was born from the realization that a connection to nature is essential for residents living in a dense industrial city. The first kleingarten was opened in 1864 by Ernst Innozenz Hauschild and named for Moritz Schreber, an influential child psychologist who had died three years earlier.[1] Today, anyone living in Germany can apply to join a garden cooperative and rent a 400-square-meter plot of their own. There are more than a million well-managed allotment gardens in Germany, and similar private and public community garden and victory garden programs exist in cities around the world.

The culture of stewardship that gardening engenders is all about intention. In collaboration with the sun, water, and minerals, and through the focused direction of our work (caloric energy) into regenerative actions — the creative production of order and beauty, the growth of nourishment — we help bring a better world into being. It is incredibly rewarding to harvest the crops of one's own labor.

How can we learn from the act of gardening as we take collective action in the context of the climate crisis? As a species, we have a duty to tend our collective garden at the scale of Earth's biosphere. Our regenerative actions must scale up and extend far beyond our garden walls. We must begin to cultivate our clean energy future with intention. Perhaps renewable energy technologies can be designed to bring us closer to nature and to each other, to cultivate beauty as cultural landscapes of energy. What might that future look like?

The Context of the Bundesgartenschau

Every other year since 1951, one winning city in Germany has had the honor of hosting the Bundesgartenschau (BUGA) — the world's most impressive horticulture festival. Many of the millions of visitors come for information they can use in their own kleingarten. The City of Mannheim hosted the festival in 1975 and was chosen for a second time to host BUGA 23.

When visitors explored the BUGA 75 event a half century ago, the world was in the midst of economic pressures resulting from a crisis in energy supplies. BUGA 23 takes place during what may be an even more pivotal moment in world history, once again related to a crisis in energy. As European economies emerge from pandemic-induced inflation, the Russian invasion of Ukraine and the sudden scarcity of oil and gas has pushed the situation to extremes. This slows the pace of climate action in the short term while reinforcing the long-term need to transition the global economy away from volatile and unpredictable fossil fuel supplies. Similar and related economic pressures are threatening the stability of established democratic institutions worldwide. Long-standing norms — even our systems of value and exchange — are being questioned in the context of a slow but steady awakening to the fundamental discordance that exists between neoliberal free market capitalism and a habitable Earth. Slowly, but surely, we are coming to see that infinite models of economic growth on a finite planet, fed by incentives of consumption, pollution, and extraction are not compatible in the long term with the cultivation of resilient, biodiverse, and thriving ecosystems upon which we rely for our survival.

How are we as citizens to respond to these multifaceted existential crises — what the historian Adam Tooze has dubbed the "global polycrisis?" How do we confront such daunting and interconnected challenges without falling into despair?

Those fortunate enough to have the respite of their gardens will continue to seek refuge there. While the environment of the garden and our activities there can be emotionally healing, perhaps there are larger lessons to be learned from the natural symbiotic systems at play in our gardens that can be applied to thriving and sustainable cities.

As Jane Jacobs writes in *The Nature of Economies*, if we can learn to understand the flow of capital and resources in human economic systems as a reflection of the flow of energy and nutrients within complex adaptive ecological systems, we can begin to design our human infrastructures to work in harmony with nature, even to regenerate nature.[2] Rather than seeing our human economy as a zero-sum competition, we can instead see it as a complex web of interactions and mutual dependencies between different subsystems where natural limits to infinite growth are an integral and beneficial feature. Through this lens, there is no disciplinary distinction to be made between economics and ecology. We can see the critical importance of our reliance on natural systems, that "biomimicry is a form of economic development," and underpinning everything is solar energy and the efficient recycling of that energy through circular metabolic processes where there is no concept of waste.

The invitation from BUGA 23 to bring the eighth Land Art Generator Initiative international design competition to Mannheim offered the rare opportunity to imagine nearly sixty hectares of land near the heart of the city. This land became available through the closing of the Spinelli Barracks, a World War II era United States Army supply and logistics base that had been closed off to the public for seventy years while also leaving a significant impact on the cultural history of the city.

The LAGI 2022 site boundary reaches into the city, recognizing the park as a point of transit and a place of convening between surrounding neighborhoods. LAGI 2022 incorporates the masterplan for the new mixed-use development around the northern edges of the park and asks what a renewable energy landscape can aspire to be in such a prominent location — where it will be seen peeking through the morning fog by nearby residents as they sip their morning coffee on balconies too small to accommodate much more than a few potted plants, or by runners maintaining their morning exercise routines.

These are the same city dwellers who might maintain their own kleingarten nearby with a small shed, fruit trees, and plenty of space to grow fresh vegetables to eat and share. LAGI 2022 Mannheim is a catalog for these gardens — a glimpse into a future world where the hundreds of millions of square meters of well-tended gardens provide gigawatt hours of green electricity to help power our cities.

The LAGI 2022 Mannheim design site includes the old U-Halle building, the terminus of an old railroad line that is no longer in service. As you learn about the design proposals you will see how some of the designers have creatively incorporated the railroad into their visions for the future of Spinelli Park, focusing their interventions at the central crossroads of the park through which the railroad line runs. With the exception of the U-Halle, the LAGI 2022 Mannheim design site is almost entirely open space, home to the protected wall lizard, brown hare, various other small mammals, many species of birds and insects, and a rich variety of wildflowers, grasses, and copses of trees.

Spinelli Park is an important component of Mannheim's North East Green Corridor Project, connecting 230 hectares of green areas forming a corridor stretching into the city center. The kilometers-long continuous stretch of green will create new places to walk, play, and relax, at the same time improving the city's air quality and climate.

Visitors to BUGA 23 will discover the complex interconnections between horticulture, land use, food security, ecosystem services, human health, climate change, renewable energy, biodiversity, and all 17 of the United Nations Sustainable Development Goals (SDGs). "Affordable and Clean Energy" is number seven on the list, but energy also has an important role to play in nearly every other SDG.

Just as energy can be found everywhere in a garden — from the photosynthesis in every leaf to the chemistry in the soil — energy's thread weaves through every aspect of human life and culture.[3] And just as energy permeates all aspects of our lives, we might consider how deeply our human culture permeates all aspects of the energy transition.

Academic literature and policy journals are replete with information about the science of the climate crisis, about the industries and nations most responsible for historic and present-day emissions, about the technical breakthroughs that are making fossil fuels obsolete, and about the socio-technical pathways that we might follow to draw down our collective impact on the environment and avoid runaway feedback loops of carbon and methane cycles. It has been well established that the technologies that are already commercialized — including solar, wind, geothermal, hydro, wave, tidal, and energy storage — can revolutionize humanity's relationship to energy and material consumption.

All we need to do is deploy these technologies. And yet it is the details and mechanisms of this deployment — the "socio" part of the socio-technical transition — that seems to be the most serious barrier to progress. So many unanswered questions are tripping us up.

[1] J. Elke Ertle, *Walled-In: A West Berlin Girl's Journey to Freedom* (Mentobe Press, 2013).

[2] Jacobs, Jane, *The Nature of Economies* (Knopf Doubleday Publishing Group, 2002).

[3] Pasqualetti, Martin J., *The Thread of Energy* (New York: Oxford Academic, 2022), https://doi.org/10.1093/oso/9780199394807.001.0001.

What communications strategies will build the strongest public support for rapid deployment? How do we maneuver around the political and media power advantages of the fossil fuel lobby? What happens to the workers in the small towns who rely on the extractive industries of the fossil fuel economy? How do we ethically extract the raw materials required for the green economy? Where exactly are these massive new solar and wind farms going to be located? Who will own them and profit from them? Do they compete with farmland or with cherished landscapes? Will they be centralized in gigawatt-scale installations, or will they be more decentralized on rooftops and parking lots? What exactly do they look like? Can we get transmission lines permitted? Do we cut down trees to install solar panels? What is the definition of a "just" transition?

Zukunftslosigkeit

As the world faces unprecedented energy challenges and with little more than a decade to act decisively on decarbonization, we seem woefully unprepared to answer the important social and cultural questions of the energy transition. We have spent so much time convincing ourselves of the science and not enough time thinking through the real-life consequences of taking the actions the science demands of us.

Consequently, the public seems ill-equipped to imagine how these changes can improve their lives and how they can contribute to the transition. For many, it seems as if the energy transition is happening "to" them and without their consultation. Suddenly, the scenery is changing. Their way of life might be next.

This makes it all too easy for fossil fuel companies to tell alarming stories of life in a world without oil and gas. These narratives are designed to build up reactionary fervor against wind and solar projects and against climate legislation at a time when we simply cannot afford to delay action. Gloom and doom narratives of climate apocalypse, environmental campaigns that focus on assigning blame, and activism that relies on shock and destruction of property may even contribute to reactionary pushback, no matter how well intended.

What is missing is an effective counter narrative that tells an inspiring story of life in a world without oil and gas. That story is better rooted in facts and science, and it's one that is yearning to be told.

What exactly is our path to a sustainable climate future? What will it be like during the journey and what will it be like when we arrive?

On the one hand, we hear of techno-utopian ideas of clean energy abundance, circular economies, and a universal decoupling of GDP from carbon emissions. We hear that "green growth" through ESG investment[4] and innovation through markets will advance the energy transition. On the other hand, we hear that the world (at least the global north) will need to experience some measure of "degrowth" to bring human economic activity back in line with the carrying capacity of Earth[5] — that we will all need to tighten our belts, especially the top one percent. Who are we to believe? What post-carbon future do we want to write? Will life in a photon culture be superior to life in a petroculture, or will it be a step backwards?

These existential questions are being asked within a polarizing political culture of alternative facts and amidst distractions of pandemics, historic inequality, neoliberal austerity, authoritarianism, culture wars, literal wars, migration and dislocation, climate disasters, and sectarian social tension. It's no surprise that we are seeing a loss in our ability to imagine a better tomorrow. And with representatives across political parties easily corrupted by money and power, it is no wonder that people are losing faith in the democratic process and institutions.

A significant segment of popular culture has been fixated on dystopian science fiction. Climate despair is on the rise. Birth rates are down radically in industrialized nations. Some couples claim runaway climate change and species collapse as reasons to abstain from having children. For the first time in modern history, we are faced with the prospect of the next generation experiencing a decline in health and standard of living. It can be discouraging to say the least. How can we see a future through this fog?

The German word for this feeling is *Zukunftslosigkeit*, which loosely translated means futurelessness. The consequence of the social condition of futurelessness is a political deficit that threatens to stall the pace of change. When we cease to have hope — cease to believe in our collective ability to design and build a better world — we stop participating in social systems. We stop voting. We withdraw into the metaverse and away from our civic responsibility. We divest from state-backed money and from the social contract. We stop trusting institutions. We poison ourselves to numb the pain. Perhaps most dangerously, we open ourselves up to the populist rhetoric of nostalgia that would seek to turn back the clock on social progress. Nostalgia is the persuasive influence that remains when we close our imaginations to what a new and better future might look like.

How do we fight back against Zukunftslosigkeit?

Perhaps we can find the answer back in our gardens. In the garden, we are reminded of our responsibility to nurture beauty, to work as stewards against entropy and decay. In the garden, we must imagine, design, prepare, and sow to realize tomorrow's harvest and bounty. A garden is about natural beauty and our desire for it.

The best defense against futurelessness may be our desire for a better world. But how do we spark that desire in the public imagination? How do we convert apathy into determination?

This is where artists and designers can be superheroes in the fight against climate change. By enticingly illustrating the beauty and bounty of a world that has moved beyond combusting dirty fossil fuels, we can free the collective imagination of the world. By designing and modeling a better future through a systems approach that includes the rights of all people and the rights of nature, artists and creatives can change the conversation from one of blame, shame, doom, and gloom to a conversation about vision, aspiration, and achievement. When people see that better future — when they really see it — and when they can place themselves and their grandchildren in it through stories told about it, then we might come together and rally behind the actions necessary to turn that vision into reality. To tell those stories, we must begin by deeply thinking about what that better future looks like — running through the details and designing it — just like we do when planning a garden.

Winning Back the Future

What does it look like when solar power is for everyone? When renewable energy is all around us? What if we started by designing solar farms for people? Or better yet, designing them with people? What does it look like when investments in renewable energy landscapes can give back more than just kilowatt-hours and can provide other meaningful social co-benefits?

Take solar power. Solar is now the cheapest form of energy on the planet and its price continues to fall. The greatest thing about solar is that it can be installed almost anywhere and at almost any scale. It can also be made to look like almost anything. It can be flexible, semi-transparent, and all the colors of the rainbow. It can share land use with buildings, shade structures, reservoirs, parks, farms, and yes, gardens.

A net-zero world will require a tripling of existing electrical generation infrastructure to meet the needs of space heating, transportation, and industry that currently relies on oil and gas. A thriving world beyond carbon may include 80 billion commercial solar modules globally — ten large PV modules for every person on the planet — a 50-fold increase over the number already installed today.

Where do they all go? We are already seeing pressures on land use. Energy developers are struggling to find new large-scale sites. Environmental laws are being weaponized against renewable energy projects. The permitting challenges faced by large-scale solar and wind farms are surpassed only by the permitting challenges facing the power transmission and distribution lines required to bring all of that power to cities. Solar energy landscapes are increasingly competing with other land use interests, such as agriculture, recreation, visual resources stewardship, land conservation, forest preservation, and biodiversity.

It is getting more difficult to get approval for renewable energy developments, with more than four out of five proposed solar projects never reaching commercial operation.[6] The reasons for withdrawal of grid interconnection requests are varied, but local objections and land use conflicts often play a role. In 2021, what was to be the United States' largest solar farm, the one-billion-dollar 850-megawatt Battle Born Solar Project, was scrapped, in part, because it would have destroyed the visual context for Michael Heizer's epic work of Land Art, *Double Negative*.[7] All across the world there are conflicts raging between farmers and solar developers that threaten to keep gigawatts of already financed projects from being deployed.

With so much pushback and local objection, it is essential that new solar installations be designed with intention, mindful of their relationship to nature, place, and people. To avoid unnecessary disruptions to deployment, we may consider "rethinking energy policy as socio-energy systems design,"[8]

[4] Environmental, Social, and Governance framework for investors. What qualifies as an ESG investment has been the subject of much debate and there is no universal standard. Companies with poor track records on environmental stewardship can often be found on ESG lists and the system has been criticized as a green washing of finance. A 2021 study of ESG funds found that many contain investments in oil, coal, gambling, alcohol, and tobacco. See: Emma Goring, "Sustainable Finance is Rife with Greenwash," *The Economist*, June 2021.

[5] See the manifesto of the *Degrowth Journal* at https://degrowthjournal.org (Timothée Parrique, founding editor).

[6] Joseph Rand, Mark Bolinger, Ryan H. Wiser, Seongeun Jeong, Bentham Paulos, "Queued Up: Characteristics of Power Plants Seeking Transmission Interconnection As of the End of 2020," *Energy Technologies Area, Berkeley Lab*, June 2021, https://eta.lbl.gov/publications/queued-characteristics-power-plants.

[7] Gabriella Angeleti, "Plans scrapped for solar project that would disrupt Michael Heizer's Double Negative," *The Art Newspaper*, July 26, 2021, https://www.theartnewspaper.com/2021/07/26/plans-scrapped-for-solar-project-that-would-disrupt-michael-heizers-double-negative.

[8] Clark A. Miller, Jennifer Richter, Jason O'Leary, "Socio-energy systems design: A policy framework for energy transitions," *Energy Research & Social Science*, Volume 6 (2015): 29–40, https://www.sciencedirect.com/science/article/abs/pii/S2214629614001236.

recognizing that technology does not live in a vacuum. The application of technology must be designed to appeal to the desires of people if it is to be deployed at scale.

The more solar generation we can bring into our cities, the more we can ease the burden on rural landscapes. According to the United States National Renewable Energy Laboratory (NREL), "The total national technical potential of rooftop PV is 1,118 GW of installed capacity."[9] To that, add the potential for photovoltaic canopies over surface parking, which covers 10,000 km² of the United States (another 1,000 GW).[10] Utilizing just half of that area would exceed the entire electrical generation capacity of the United States in 2023. In other words, the available area in cities is powerful.

This book — and the designs it illustrates from hundreds of creatives around the world — supports this kind of radical decentralization of our energy landscapes. It proposes that we imagine going even further to bring renewable energy into the spaces between buildings and begin to energize the public realm.

Designing and Owning Together

As we work to decarbonize the world over the next two decades, we will be faced with many challenges when it comes to the acceptance of new solar and wind projects.

Early and consistent community engagement throughout the design process will become increasingly important, especially for installations within or near to population centers. Answering the questions of where we should install renewable energy, who will be impacted by the installations, and who will benefit from them are fundamental to the success of the energy transition. No one today can guess the eventual mix of urban versus rural energy generation, but we know that the more we can decentralize through distributed energy resources, the more reliable and affordable our clean energy future will be.

What are the social and cultural ramifications that follow from prioritizing a decentralized grid? How can cities and towns take advantage of the opportunity to deploy solar energy inside their own boundaries in ways that enhance not only urban sustainability but also urban livability, resilience, beauty, food security, racial and economic justice, and economic development? These co-benefits make the prospect of the energy transition an exciting and potentially transformational investment for municipalities, electric utilities, foundations, and others looking for ways to leverage social innovation and socially responsible investment to create better futures.

How can coordinated city-wide solar projects enhance local culture, enliven public spaces, and provide other extensive co-benefits? Can urban solar innovation benefit economically disadvantaged communities or help reverse historical patterns of urban racial and economic injustice? Are there ways of aggregating rooftops, public spaces, empty lots, brownfield sites, parking lots, and other viable sites within the city to create large-scale urban projects for procurement, taking advantage of similar economies of scale as large rural projects? What kinds of financing mechanisms could be developed to expand the pool of investors and beneficiaries? Can the universal resource of solar energy be managed in such a way as to accrue benefits universally to all people? How will these new infrastructures be culturally and aesthetically integrated into urban visualscapes and enhance the public commons?

Providing carbon-free energy in the fight against climate change is the most obvious benefit of solar power. What may be overlooked are the benefits of distributed solar for local economies and as a mechanism to increase social equity and quality of life. Properly planned and implemented, city-integrated solar infrastructure can provide a wide array of co-benefits.

Energy developers can learn from best practices for community-centered design within the fields of architecture, landscape architecture, and urban design. By co-designing energy landscapes with the people who live in proximity to them, we can increase urban solar integration, preserve remote landscapes, and help to accelerate a transition to an energy system that works in harmony with the environment.

Participatory design practice for energy development can also ensure a more just and equitable clean energy future by leveraging the many co-benefits of solar power infrastructure when it shares land uses with parks, gardens, canals, riverfronts, and streetscapes. The wealth of proven technologies for aesthetic solar photovoltaic integration within architecture and landscape architecture offers a path to implementation for a far more ambitious deployment of distributed energy within cities than is ordinarily considered by urban planners, real estate developers, and energy developers.

The application of solar infrastructure can increase the energy independence of municipalities. Cities are already taking advantage of long-term power purchase agreements for clean energy to establish pricing stability. By bringing solar installations into urban neighborhoods, cities can accomplish the same goal while also contributing to resilience and efficiency by limiting reliance on monopoly utilities and eliminating maintenance costs for remote distribution infrastructures. Localized supply chains can emerge to provide good paying jobs while decreasing the embodied environmental footprint of solar modules.

The Solar Energy Commons

The energy of the sun is a universal natural resource. Throughout history there are examples of a "universal property" approach to the distribution of natural resource benefits. The most often cited example is the Alaska Permanent Fund. Writing in *Scientific American*, James Boyce summarizes the program:

> In 1976, as oil production commenced on Alaska's North Slope, the state amended its constitution to create a new entity called the Alaska Permanent Fund. The idea was the brainchild of Republican governor Jay Hammond, who believed that Alaska's oil wealth belonged to all its residents, and that all should receive equal annual dividends from its extraction.[11]

The idea extends to the principle of the "solar energy commons," a recognition that the sun's energy belongs to all of us if it belongs to any of us. Much like the social benefits that can be found from community gardens that share the dividends of solar energy across arable landscapes, community solar projects can be a way to invest in shared prosperity. Especially when installed on public land or community land trusts, solar power offers an opportunity for an equitable distribution of a solar dividend — a policy mechanism that can be a powerful tool to combat the cycles of poverty experienced by so many the world over. The sale of solar electricity from public projects could pay out a universal dividend[12] and provide new opportunities for private wealth generation through distributed energy ownership, a democratization of what is today almost entirely monopoly ownership.

Technologies, such as virtual net metering, make it possible for individuals to become energy "prosumers" selling kilowatt-hours directly peer-to-peer (P2P). As privatization of solar infrastructure becomes more widespread, it will be important to make sure that the financial benefits of these new capital investment opportunities are not limited to the upper class, but intentionally provide diversity of ownership as a means to close the wealth gap.

As we look to a future of greater distributed solar energy deployment, we can think of "renewable cities" as those that have installed within the city limits at least one solar module per city resident, that source all of their energy from renewable sources, and that support the option of thriving, car-free lifestyles. Renewable cities will have major competitive advantages over non-renewable ones. They will tend to be more livable, equitable, innovative, and resilient — qualities that make for strong economic development. Replacing fossil fuel infrastructure in cities improves air quality and quality of life, among the myriad of co-benefits of installing a significant number of solar panels within the city.

Solar panels installed over community gardens and urban farms can collect rainwater for irrigation and increase crop yields, radically conserving water by strategically shading crops while contributing to food security. This type of land use sharing between energy and food production has come to be known delightfully as "agrivoltaics."

Solar panels installed over canals and reservoirs can radically improve water conservation by decreasing evaporation. The water, in turn, helps to keep the solar modules cool and operating efficiently. This type of solar installation is often referred to as "floatovoltaics."

Solar panels installed as shading devices in public spaces can help reduce heat island effects, creating cool microclimates and lowering the risk of heat stroke in summer. Solar can help define walking and biking paths, rights-of-way, and waterfronts while protecting people from the elements. Community solar can be used as a placemaking tool, adding value to civic parks. We can call this type of solar installation "communivoltaics," which can be seen as an extension of rooftop solar into the public realm and the commons.

Perhaps most powerfully, when creative community members get involved in the design process, solar power plants can become works of art in public space. In this way, some element of our clean energy infrastructure can help turn our urban and suburban landscapes into energy sculpture parks. Such multifaceted investment in a post-carbon future supports culture and makes our cities more livable as they become more sustainable, equitable, and resilient.

[9] Pieter Gagnon, Robert Margolis, Caleb Phillips, "Rooftop Photovoltaic Technical Potential in the United States," *U.S. Department of Energy Office of Scientific and Technical Information*, November 5, 2019, https://www.osti.gov/biblio/1575064.

[10] Daniel Herriges, "Parking Dominates Our Cities. But Do We Really See It?," *Strong Towns*, November 27, 2019, https://www.strongtowns.org/journal/2019/11/27/parking-dominates-our-cities-but-do-we-really-see-it.

[11] James K. Boyce. "The Case for Universal Property." *Scientific American*, November 28, 2020, https://www.scientificamerican.com/article/the-case-for-universal-property.

[12] Robert Stayton, *Solar Dividends—How Solar Energy can Generate a Basic Income for Everyone on Earth*, (Santa Cruz: Sandstone, 2019).

Sowing the Seeds of Desire

If we truly want the massive change we know must be achieved in the face of climate risks, we can take lessons from Madison Avenue and focus communication strategies on desire and human ambition. Oil companies and automakers do it. They convince people of how great life is in a petroculture. They illustrate the freedom of the open road. They don't scare people into driving internal combustion engine cars or shame them into buying disposable plastic stuff. They tempt them. Likewise, climate action must be at least as tempting.

It is true that we live in a time of crisis. Yet the future is full of promise. Designers and artists have the ability to manifest that promise by inspiring collective action through their imaginations and the stories they tell about the greatness of our future.

As you peruse the concepts and technologies incorporated into the artwork proposals on the pages of this book, try to look past the climate change arguments of the past three decades. Put aside your despair about a bleak future and toss off your thoughts of doom and gloom. Instead, imagine yourself walking through these artful energy landscapes, enjoying a day in the park in a world that has long since moved beyond burning fossil fuels for energy. It's a world with more bird song drifting in the fresh, clean air — a world in which cities mostly power themselves locally with some help from remote wind turbines and solar farms. In this world, a circular economy means the end of waste streams and no more extraction of non-renewable raw materials. Energy dividends of solar power increase the quality of life for everyone and support a rich and diverse economy.

Imagine yourself in Spinelli Park a few years from now, walking through *Energy Circus* — a kind of living history museum of the future demonstrating agrivoltaic gardens and a circular economy. Or imagine yourself resting beneath the soft shade of *Plane of Water* as wildflowers blossom around you, lush from the water the artwork provides. What would it be like to take in a performance at *Kaleidoscopic Dunes* one evening, knowing that the pavilion generated 250 kWh of electricity that day?

A sense of desire for a better world like the one these artworks point to is the motivation that will successfully drive the massive change we need. The artists and designers featured in this book hold the keys to unlock that desire.

The LAGI 2022 artworks open our eyes to the possibility of an end to scarcity and a future of shared prosperity maintained within the carrying capacity of Earth. They remind us that with today's technology we could live in a 100% renewable energy-powered circular economy. Through art, we are allowed to inhabit the future. We can see ourselves there. We can see our children there.

It's time to tell a new and inspiring climate story — a narrative that moves beyond the doom and gloom of what will happen if we don't act. We can instead paint a detailed picture of the life-affirming, equitable, and thriving world we will create through our collective action. This story is about the quality of life and the experiences of those who will live their lives in this better world.

LAGI 2022 Mannheim offered an opportunity to tell this story. The artists, designers, and writers in this collection answered the call. Now it is your turn to tell the story to others. Together, let's design our clean energy infrastructures to be reflections of our greatest selves — to be places that make our lives meaningful and wonderful.

As the educational component of LAGI 2022 Mannheim, we designed and produced a new game called *Kleingarten*. Our second collaboration with Tunnel Monster Collective, this new roll-and-write game is a fun way to learn about the interconnected systems at work within a 400 square meter allotment garden. Players build features and share harvest with neighbors on their way to becoming a master grower.

Energy Circus

Chai Yi Yang

See page 50

Plane of Water

Zsuzsa Péter

See page 68

Kaleidoscopic Dune

Muny-Roth Chev, Jason Daniel, Vatsapol Nanta

See page 56

LAGI 2022 MANNHEIM DESIGN GUIDELINES

Projects must

Create a three dimensional outdoor human space using one or more renewable energy technologies as the predominant sculptural media;

Be considered from a perspective of modularity and/or scalability in order to address both civic and residential scales as;

Be safe for people by housing power electronics and energy storage systems away from easy access;

Seek to inspire people about the beauty of renewable energy and bring a positive message about life in a post-carbon future;

Help to advance one or more of the 17 UN Sustainable Development Goals;

Fit within the design site boundary area, illustrating beautiful energy generation capacity for both private garden and civic park;

Provide social co-benefits through the design including but not limited to urban farming, gardening, recreation, education, public engagement, interactivity, play, energy security, and economic opportunities;

Not generate greenhouse gas emissions or other forms of environmental pollution;

Each entry must provide a brief (approximately 300 words) environmental assessment as a part of the written description in order to determine the effects of the project on natural ecosystems and to outline a strategy to mitigate any foreseeable issues;

Be informed by an understanding of the history and surrounding context of the design site;

Support the objectives of the Climate Corridor (Klimopass), a component of the Baden-Württemberg climate adaptation plan;

The Climate Corridor is intended to allow fresh air to flow unobstructed into the city. Therefore your proposal should not create an impediment to the flow of air; and

Be pragmatic and constructible, employing technology that can be scalable and tested. There is no limit on the type of technology or the proprietary nature of the technology that is specified.

The LAGI 2022 Mannheim design site boundary invited creatives to imagine a renewable energy design across multiple scales.

At the civic park scale is the vast landscape recently made available in the City of Mannheim following the closing of the U.S. military's Spinelli Barracks. The land has been remediated and the space will open to the public during BUGA 23. Following the Bundesgartenschau, the site will become primarily a public park—a gateway to the Rhine-Neckar Climate Corridor—and may incorporate a productive energy landscape that can significantly contribute to Mannheim's renewable energy generation capacity. Creatives were invited to design an energy landscape as a public park.

On the other end of the scale spectrum we asked that some element of the design proposal fit beautifully to power a private garden. The German Schrebergarten is a small plot of land that provides opportunity for urban dwellers to engage with nature and grow ornamental or edible gardens.

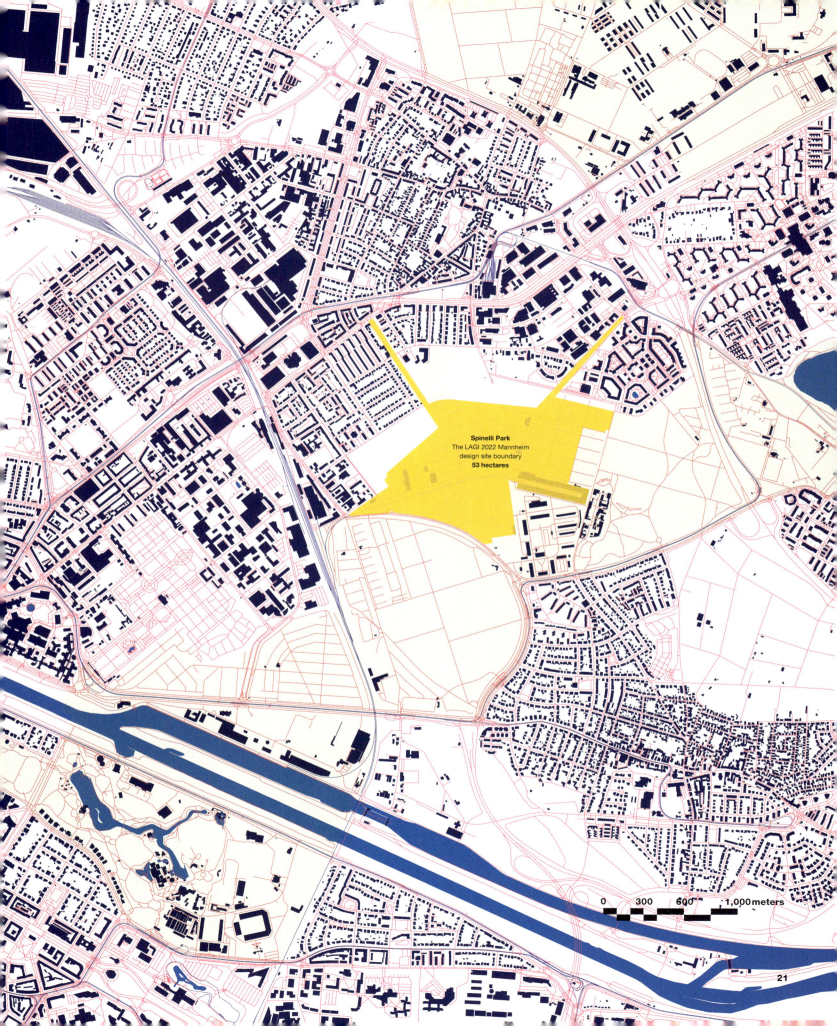

RHINE-NECKAR CLIMATE CORRIDOR

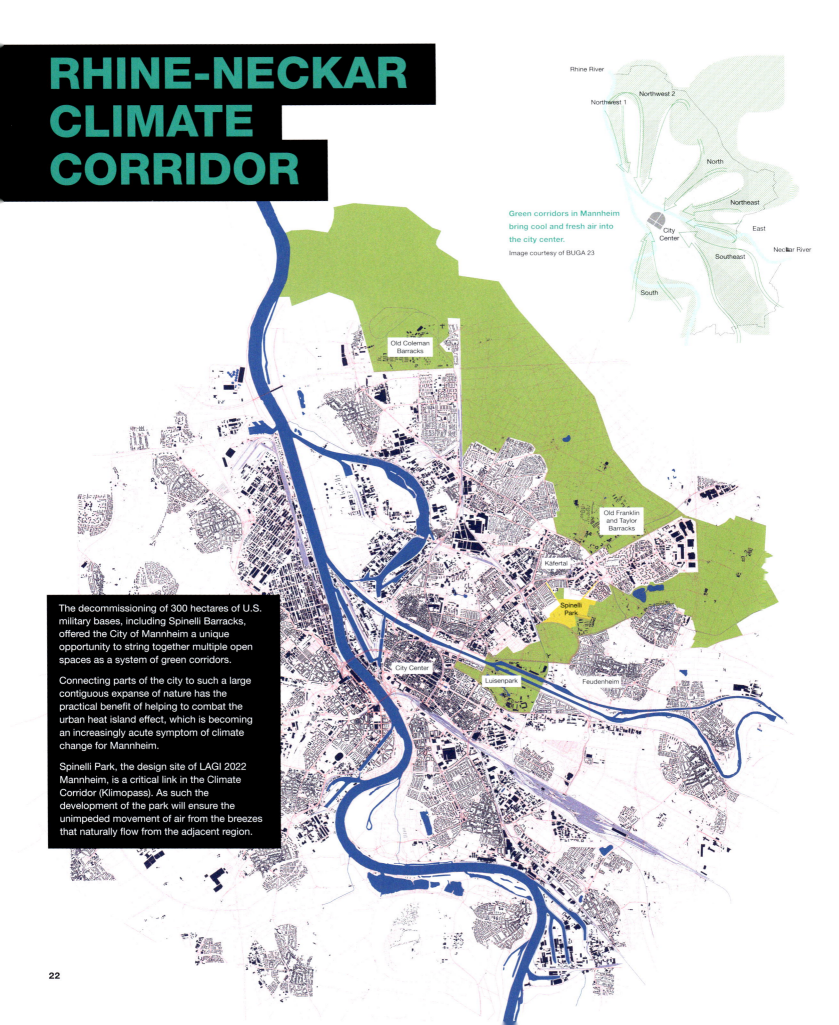

Green corridors in Mannheim bring cool and fresh air into the city center.
Image courtesy of BUGA 23

The decommissioning of 300 hectares of U.S. military bases, including Spinelli Barracks, offered the City of Mannheim a unique opportunity to string together multiple open spaces as a system of green corridors.

Connecting parts of the city to such a large contiguous expanse of nature has the practical benefit of helping to combat the urban heat island effect, which is becoming an increasingly acute symptom of climate change for Mannheim.

Spinelli Park, the design site of LAGI 2022 Mannheim, is a critical link in the Climate Corridor (Klimapass). As such the development of the park will ensure the unimpeded movement of air from the breezes that naturally flow from the adjacent region.

Above: Former train access to the Spinelli site. **Below:** Water basin on the Spinelli site.
Photographs © BUGA 23/Daniel Lukac

View of the Spinelli site
Photographs © BUGA 23/Daniel Lukac

View of the Spinelli site
Photograph © BUGA 23/Daniel Lukac

ESSAY

The Becoming of Spinelli

Tina Nailor
LAGI 2022 Mannheim Project Manager

Introduction

From agricultural fields to military barracks to a keystone of green urbanism, the contemporary Spinelli Park has a fascinating story to tell. Its history is a journey of contrasting urban landscapes and cultures — the estrangement of a large parcel of land from its surrounding city and from its citizens who were denied access for generations. And yet it is also a narrative of collaboration, of German American partnerships, and a friendship that remains celebrated in Mannheim's identity to inform a vision for a sustainable and equitable future. This transformation is inspiring Mannheim's approach to mitigating climate change and connecting communities by reestablishing pathways through inclusive spaces — reconnecting a lost parcel with the people who were refused memories of this place for so long. Spinelli's re-integration into Mannheim's urban fabric is part of an interdisciplinary strategy of extensive urban planning for a future post-carbon city.

Mannheim is a city nestled between the rivers Rhine (Rhein in German) and Neckar in southwest Germany. The Rhine-Neckar region has provided vital infrastructure for Mannheim to grow its industry and economy through innovations such as the invention of the automobile (Karl-Benz) and the bicycle, even the tractor. A thriving economy has shaped the landscape, infrastructure, and its role in industrial progress since the early 1800s.[1] Such progress and location became vital in military strategies during WWII, which can be witnessed today in Mannheim's urban surroundings. Part of these landscapes are former U.S. military sites. One of these sites is the Spinelli Barracks, which is one of five former U.S. military compounds in Mannheim that were established after WWII. Together they occupied a total of 530.4 hectares within Mannheim city limits and influenced Mannheim's urban growth pattern and cultural development.[2] These landscapes have cultural and environmental impacts that resonate with Mannheim's vision for the future, turning what was once a limitation into an opportunity for inclusive housing, hosting the 2023 German Federal Garden Show (BUGA 23), and climate mitigation through the sustainable urban planning of the Northeast Green Corridor (Grünzug Nordost).

Historic Building Blocks

To better understand the specific characteristics of Spinelli and its role in future city planning we must refer to the past, upon which the foundation for the legacy of German and American coexistence and partnership was laid.

Before the site became known as Spinelli, it was the Pionie Kaserne, which housed the Pionier Batallion 33 for the German Wehrmacht on a forty-hectare area in Mannheim-Feudenheim.[3] On March 29, 1945, the U.S. military crossed the Rhine and occupied Mannheim. They quickly established a footing through Mannheim's existing German barracks in and around the city.[4] Later, the Mannheim region became a central part of the U.S. allied zones by connecting and expanding these former German military bases. Each U.S. military barracks became a node in a military mobility system, moving and processing vital elements across a wide network. This evolved into an interconnected infrastructure of Mannheim-U.S. garrisons comprising Coleman, Franklin, Taylor, and Spinelli Barracks, and connecting with the existing highways, railroads, and waterways embedded in the Mannheim landscape. In November 1945, 800 U.S. soldiers were stationed at Spinelli Barracks, which continued to grow into the Combat Equipment Group Europe (CEGE) composed of eighty hectares and a military community of over a thousand U.S. military personnel, U.S. civilians, and German civilians throughout the years.[5]

On May 31, 1945, Mannheim became a logistics hub for all military equipment maintenance and storage in Europe. Expanding the military buildup through existing infrastructure and the spatial mechanism of military bases, such as Spinelli, increased Mannheim's central role in the military supply chain of Europe. Spinelli Barrack's main role was to support U.S. deployment and redeployment of U.S. military forces through logistics and supply up until the final withdrawal in 2015 through the U.S. Base Realignment and Closure Act (BRAC).[6] During this 70-year period, more than 500,000 Americans came to Mannheim and shared their culture, traditions, and stories. These lives have blended into Mannheim's regionalism and identity and continue to echo through the alliances and collaboration of community partnerships and friendships.

"Spinelli is more than an extraordinary example of land use and development. Its history and integration are a reminder of how we as a society are deeply rooted in the land that shapes our identity and environment. This connection is the catalyst for Mannheim's sustainable planning and community, focusing on the present and future vision to move forward into a greener future of a carbon neutral city."

— Tina Nailor

ESSAY

Cultivating Photovoltaics for Producing Beauty

Alessandra Scognamiglio
Architect, Senior Researcher at the National Agency for New Technologies, Energy and Sustainable Economic Development (ENEA)

As photovoltaic installations increase in capacity from kilowatts to megawatts and even gigawatts, their impact on landscapes becomes more top of mind to governing bodies and to a larger portion of the public. With a wide array of stakeholders, addressing the impacts of solar energy landscapes requires economic, ecological, but also aesthetic and cultural studies of proposed projects, along with considered landscape design and planning to harmonize all of these interests.

Solar energy landscapes are too often perceived as industrial intrusions detrimental to the cultural value of the landscape — a highly visible and unfortunately necessary response to the mostly invisible threat of climate change. As a consequence, local authorities and communities often oppose the implementation of photovoltaics, because they are not aware of the co-benefits to the local economy and ecology. For example, biodiversity may be maintained and even augmented by the partial shade that solar panels provide. The efficient use of water for irrigation can be improved when plants are not exposed to direct sun through long summer days. This symbiotic relationship between energy production and food production offers consequential benefits to farmers, but a lack of awareness of these benefits leads to categorical dismissal of solar projects in some jurisdictions.

To reduce this type of local opposition, new models for development that engage the public and offer a more expansive suite of co-benefits can support the design of beautiful photovoltaic systems. Exemplary projects can be perceived as positive additions to the landscape.

Solar power is already acknowledged as the cheapest technology in history for generating electricity, as confirmed by the International Energy Agency (IEA World Energy Outlook 2020). While solar's declining cost curve is absolutely to be celebrated, the race to the cheapest kilowatt-hour has created some challenges. New visions are needed for beautifying twenty-first century cultural landscapes that include photovoltaic systems.

The challenge is to think about photovoltaic arrays as design elements of landscapes, rather than exclusively as power plants — as machines for energy. Instead, we have the opportunity during this most important stage in the energy transition to transform a matter of technology into a matter of culture. This transformation of framing is made possible by the versatility and flexibility of solar technologies. We now have on offer a varied set of design possibilities to master this challenge and produce beauty by using solar technology as a medium for creativity.

The existing binaries that result from siloed thinking — photovoltaics versus visual landscape or photovoltaics versus cropland — keep us from thinking about what collective good can come from a transdisciplinary approach to the design process of energy landscapes. Edgar Morin identifies transdisciplinarity as the main tool for tackling the wicked complexities of the polycrisis of our age.[1]

Why are photovoltaics so often perceived as a threat to the landscape?

The most common reaction is negative because photovoltaics are generally perceived as an intruder into the landscape. A large photovoltaic system, with its vast blue areas of photovoltaic modules, makes energy production visible to nearby communities. This is something new, in contrast to traditional fossil fuels where the site of production is generally far away from the vast majority of people. The climate impacts of coal-fired power plants are global, but their immediate pollution effects on the visual landscape and on air and water quality are limited to the unfortunate communities directly downstream. Many of those who benefit from the electricity generated from a coal-fired power plant are blissfully unaware of its impacts.

Visual perception accounts for 80% of the total perception. In this sense, the perception of photovoltaics as an intruder is hard to avoid. By the nature of the technology, solar energy landscapes happen to be highly visual and large objects, but they are not designed as such. The mainstream design approach is predominantly the utilitarian engineering approach — optimizing the energy and economic performance while overlooking the visual performance.

Large ground-mounted arrays in greenfields are the lowest cost design solution for installing solar and account for the majority of installations. A typical large-scale photovoltaic array is characterized by a standard visual configuration.

Within the area occupied by the photovoltaic array, parallel rows of modules are installed with their azimuth and tilt angles optimized for the latitude of the site. A minimum space between rows avoids shading effects and facilitates maintenance operations.

It is easy to observe that photovoltaic arrays, designed in this way, are self-referential or without context. They do not suit the features of the landscape within which they exist in at least three ways. First, the land area occupied by the system can be too large with respect to the other elements of the landscape. Second, the orientation of the modules toward the sun (south in the Northern Hemisphere and north in the Southern Hemisphere) determines a pattern of installation with a single predominant direction — namely east-west — determined by the parallel rows. This can be striking with respect to the other geometric features of the landscape. Third, the density of the photovoltaic pattern is often incompatible with the landscape pattern, evoking a strong sense of artificiality.

As a consequence of this design model, areas occupied by standard photovoltaic systems can be perceived as stolen from the landscape. They are often striking, and no function besides energy generation can take place in the same area of land. Their most obvious characteristic is that of technological objects superimposed on the agrarian landscape as an industrial monoculture.

If the pattern of a standard photovoltaic system is a given, this does not imply that it cannot be designed with an additional intention. Sharing land uses with solar energy can open up opportunities for creativity, social and cultural benefits, and enhanced biodiversity. If any change with respect to the standard pattern implies a loss in energy generation, this may be more than offset by the co-benefits offered by improved visual performance.

The photovoltaic pattern can be designed as a part of the landscape pattern, by conceiving a three-dimensional spatial configuration of the modules, designed to include integrated functions and performative spaces.

The *Solar Strand*, designed by Walter Hood and realized at the Buffalo University Campus in 2010, uses the dimensions and spacing of the photovoltaic modules to set up recreational spaces that people can enjoy. By lifting the modules slightly off the ground, the local grassland ecosystem is allowed to thrive.

The mindset shift represented by the *Solar Strand* is possible when the design focus moves from photovoltaic technology to the quality of the space that the modules are able to shape through their physical form.

A conventional engineering process focuses on the figural elements — the photovoltaic modules and their technical components. In the *Solar Strand*, the attention is more toward the space that is created in between and underneath the photovoltaic modules. Japanese culture defines this as "Ma" (間), the negative space in between. This void becomes ripe with possibilities.

Beauty is the pattern which connects,[2] and the void is where connections take place. Therefore, in the case of photovoltaics, the design of 間 — the empty space full of possibilities — is the key for producing beauty (connections) while also producing energy.

The shape that photovoltaic modules give to the space in between and to the ground plane beneath their surfaces should be considered during the early design process for their ability to create connections between the technological system and the landscape, including humans, flora, and fauna. This upturning of perspective allows for the necessary shift from a mere energy transition to a cultural transition, where photovoltaic systems can be seen as designed spaces allowing people to experience a new kind of landscape. From a practical perspective, this approach to deployment may serve to accelerate the renewable energy transition as more people become accepting of the technology or even come to desire its application in their community for the benefits it brings beyond kilowatt-hours.

A concrete example of this perspective is the combination of food and energy production, through agrivoltaics. Agrivoltaics offers a unique occasion to experience the negative space, which is exactly where the crops are situated. It opens a new perspective on an integrated design approach. There are several agrivoltaic configurations, the most common of which places crops between strips of modules and suspends photovoltaic modules up from the ground at a height of between three and five meters. This leaves room enough for sunlight to pass between the strips of modules and reach the ground.

Agrivoltaic systems shape a space that is conceived for growing food, allowing farmers to work in this space. In contrast to standard photovoltaic systems, they naturally integrate the continuous presence of humans. The consideration of energy landscapes that are intended to be occupied is one of the most important steps to freeing them from the common perception that they are cold and utilitarian.

[1] Edgar Morin, *La Tête Bien Faite: Repenser la Réforme, Réformer la Pensée*, (Seuil, 1999).

[2] Gregory Bateson, *Steps to an Ecology of Mind: Collected Essays in Anthropology, Psychiatry, Evolution, and Epistemology*, (University of Chicago Press, 2000).

[3] Massimo Venturi Ferriolo, *Oltre il Giardino: Filosofia di Paesaggio*, (Vele, 2019).

Agrivoltaics shapes a space for people to engage in farming activities, while the empty space is also available for other activities. The negative space can host habitats for pollinators and provide grasslands for grazing. With some design forethought, it is also possible to conceive of additional activities for humans in the space between and underneath photovoltaic modules.

By pushing the process of design further, agrivoltaic systems can be seen as a resource for communities, going beyond the productive value of electricity and agriculture, to also add social and recreational value. The key is to design agrivoltaic systems as part of the landscape first and foremost. Additionally, co-design processes can empower the local population to participate in the sustainable transformation of their landscapes. For example, in cases where agrivoltaic systems are created near urban centers, there are copious design opportunities to provide citizens with usable spaces for outdoor recreational activities. This shift is from agrivoltaic systems to "agrivoltaic gardens."

In Northern Italy, between Milan and Pavia, the NeoruraleHub project aims to address soil depletion in the Po River Valley. Intensive industrial agriculture has left the ground dry and lacking in minerals. NeoruraleHub created a model of re-naturalization, which was initially applied to four hundred hectares of land, predominantly covered by rice paddies, but which quickly grew to a thousand hectares — a feat that earned the project recognition as a Fondo Ambiente Italiano (Italian Environment Fund) site in 2019. A design by architect Fabiano Spano and Studio Alami, *A-Grid*, was chosen in 2022 for agrivoltaic development on 80 hectares of rice farm in the NeoruraleHub landscape. The selected project is the result of an invited competition organized by ENEA, the Italian National Agency for New Technologies, Energy and Sustainable Economic Development.

Agrivoltaic projects like *A-Grid* and the results of the LAGI 2022 Mannheim design competition illustrate that we are ready to think of photovoltaic fields as gardens. We are ready to embrace an "image and metaphor of living in harmony in order to prepare for a relationship that must be rethought between people, animals, and nature."[3]

Thinking of a photovoltaic field as a garden is a way to recover the complete human spirit of living, where utility and beauty coexist in reinforcing harmony. It is a way to develop visions for new cultural landscapes of the twenty-first century.

A-Grid, by Studio Alami, will be installed in 2023 on an agricultural landscape in Northern Italy.

Image © Fabiano Spano and Studio Alami

Byron Kominek's farm near Boulder, Colorado produces more than 8,000 pounds of produce every year. The solar modules generate enough power for 300 local homes while reducing irrigation water consumption by as much as half.
Photograph courtesy of Kirk Siegler/NPR

ESSAY

Unexpected Encounters with a Garden Gnome

Sven Stremke
Wageningen University, The Netherlands

Renewable energy can be beautiful. This short but intriguing sentence has been the tagline of the Land Art Generator Initiative since its founding in 2008. The idea that renewable energy can be beautiful may be matter of course to many readers and yet it remains to be fully realized at a significant scale. This suggests that today renewable energy is not always beautiful. In fact, renewable energy technologies are often considered cold and utilitarian artifacts of our living environment. This situation leaves the inspired reader with several choices.

One option is to search for evidence in the realm of energy — to visit the beautiful energy landscapes that were built in the past and that illustrate the human capacity to unite functionality and aesthetics. Think about the Hoover Dam in the United States[1] and the Solbergfoss hydropower plant in Norway, both exhibiting great attention to aesthetics — from the setting of these technical structures within the sublime host landscape, to the beautiful Art Deco penstock towers designed by Los Angeles based architect Gordon Kaufmann and the magnificent woodwork by some unknown but very talented carpenter from southern Norway.

There are other examples, of course, and some far more recent, but it has been argued that these more beautiful renewable energy landscapes are exceptions to the common practice of exploiting renewable energy sources in a purely utilitarian fashion. Is this an inconvenient truth? Must we resign ourselves to a renewable energy future of visual monotony imposed upon our viewsheds, or can we expect more beauty to emerge from our energy landscapes going forward, driven by projects that include community in the design process?

Rather than speculating about the role of avant-garde projects in the mainstreaming of innovation, I would like first to draw your attention to another ingenious process of placemaking that originated one hundred and fifty years ago in a very different domain. It is a beautiful spatial concept that is so self-evident and common today that we have almost forgotten how innovative it was. We can also explore its potential to support our pursuit of renewable energy that can be beautiful. This specific human invention continues to transcend the dichotomy of functionality and beauty, of production and joy.

Experts are still debating whether the German physician Moritz Schreber should be recognized as the inventor of the so-called allotment (UK) or community (U.S.) garden, often referred to as a Schrebergarten in Germany in his honor. What is indisputable is that millions of people around the world draw benefits today from these gardens that combine joy with food production.

In the mid-nineteenth century, people were mostly cramped in poorly ventilated cities, air quality was low, and good-quality food was scarce. Above all, urban dwellers missed contact with nature and space to play and exercise. This was Schreber's contribution at the dawn of the Industrial Revolution, demonstrating how a connection to nature can provide a pathway to self-actualization and happiness. Today's Schrebergärten, also known as allotment gardens, allow each gardener — including those who live in small urban apartments — to create their own beautiful environment. When aggregated together, these gardens become the green-blue networks that our cities continue to rely upon for maintaining biodiversity, groundcover, and healthy soils. In fact, allotment gardens are indispensable components of today's urban fabric to improve air quality, mitigate heat stress, and provide local organic food to meet an increasing demand.

But we are not revisiting the concept of allotment garden for those obvious contributions to quality of life. Rather, we are drawing inspiration from the capacity of allotment gardens to unify the seemingly irreconcilable worlds of production and joy. Or, like ecosystem services experts would argue, the capacity of the living environment to provision cultural services in addition to services of clean air, water, carbon sequestration, and natural habitat. The garden per se can serve as a powerful archetype for the energy transition. Particularly, the allotment garden that is commonly governed by elected representatives and cultivated by individual gardeners may provide inspiration and insights to those pursuing energy transition in denser populated settlements.

In Germany today, there exists about 1.4 million allotment gardens. Each gardener can become an active agent making renewable energy beautiful, and some do so already. The 470 square kilometers of German allotment gardens have the potential to not only provide renewable energy to all the families who maintain them, but also to illustrate through experimentation how a changing climate presents a nucleus for socio-technical innovation. Any such development, it must be mentioned, relies on human ingenuity and design thinking in combination with a changing worldview — one in which we finally take charge of and responsibility for the consequences of our collective behavior on the global climate, social justice, and planetary biodiversity.

What then are the tangible learnings we can draw from the millions of allotment gardens around the world and the great many passionate gardeners that cultivate those spaces?[2] What are the ingredients we can borrow for a successful transition to beautiful energy landscapes?

To start, the term "beauty" deserves some attention as it can be understood in many ways. Taken through the lens of the allotment garden, the meaning of beauty perhaps becomes easier to define. Allotment gardeners enjoy a certain degree of freedom as to what they can do within their plot. General rules, such as the minimum share of land allotted to food production, are established by the governing body for each specific allotment garden. This is where an important insight for the transition to renewable energy starts to be mirrored in the policies of governing authorities — providing clear targets and directions without hampering the site-specific and normative implementation of technologies, such as the harvesting of food or renewable energy. Beauty, in other words, not only lies in the eye of the observer but is also a function of the freedom provided to maneuver and make your own decisions.

Allotment gardeners take pride in what they do — the beauty they create within their confined spaces and the fruits they harvest in their gardens. In allotment gardens, one can find close communities of gardeners that are dedicated to the same ends. At the very least, they all find some meaning in the act of gardening. This specific means of cultivating the land, clearly visible to any visitor, is a cultural endeavor and continues to escape the tiresome chase for economic profits that dominate so many other land uses. This passion for gardening goes hand in hand with the wish to interact with others. Innovative solutions, such as solar hot water heaters, travel fast due to the continuous exchange among gardeners within one garden community and between allotment gardens. Another contributor to the high permeability of innovation are dedicated events, such as the Federal Horticultural Shows (BUGA) and the International Building Exhibitions (IBA) in Germany, The Floriade in the Netherlands, and World Expos that cultivate knowledge and pride about those everyday environments beloved by many. In Germany, the garden gnome is perhaps the best-known ambassador for the self-conception and the (admittedly at-times exaggerated) autonomy of allotment gardeners. These gnomes — small in size but powerful in terms of meaning — emblematize this fascinating type of urban fabric. Rest assured, this essay by no means intends to diminish the subcultures that have originated in some allotment gardens. They are all expressions of pride, community, and ownership, which brings us to the next learning for the transition to beautiful renewable energy.

The importance of ownership can be considered the third learning from allotment gardens — not literal, legal ownership, because most allotment gardeners lease their plot of land from public authorities, but another kind of ownership that has many ties with stewardship of the commons. Together, allotment gardeners steward a large piece of land and individual actions, such as the cultivation of vegetables, falls within the agreed-upon uses of that land. The ownership that one encounters in many allotment gardens and the great care with which the public spaces are looked after — as trivial and antiquated they may appear at first glance — provide ample opportunities to learn and apply this model to the energy transition. In other words, temporary ownership can go along with responsible and thoughtful stewardship. This finding is particularly interesting as many spaces of renewable energy generation (ground-mounted solar power plants for example) are considered cooperatively owned phenomena too.

The next set of success factors are spatial in nature. The first one concerns the physical distance between the main residence and the allotment garden. Allotment gardens are in spatial proximity to where people live and work. Virtually all allotment gardens can be reached by foot, bicycle, public transport, or short car ride. There is simply no such thing as traveling long distances to reach your allotment garden. Spatial proximity is a key property of allotment gardens and inscribed in the DNA of allotment gardeners. No one would entertain the idea of having to travel a few hours to harvest some cucumbers.

Accessibility is the second spatial denominator of allotment gardens. In fact, access to the grounds is organized very distinctively. The allotment garden as a whole is open to the public, and visitors can enjoy some of the benefits of this large piece of green infrastructure (not the aforementioned cucumber of course, which is reserved for the gardener who nurtured the plant). All allotment gardens are subdivided into plots each of which is "owned" by a gardener, while the pathways that interconnect those plots, the playgrounds, and other social gathering spaces are accessible to the public. At times, overly

[1] The editors recognize that: "Hoover Dam is a settler-colonial project, requiring Indigenous land and waterways while producing energy that enables further non-Indigenous settlement. In addition to the Dam's engineering feats, its cultural production — art, pageantry, commemoration, and media — helped to buttress these claims to land." Jane Griffith, "Hoover Damn: Land, Labor, and Settler Colonial Cultural Production." *Cultural Studies <-> Critical Methodologies*, 17(1), 30–40, https://doi.org/10.1177/1532708616640012.

[2] In the city of Mannheim, more than 6,000 gardeners maintain 25 allotment garden collectives (Wikipedia).

[3] For example, the solar power plant "de Kwekerij" in The Netherlands. See: Dirk Oudes, Sven Stremke, "Next Generation Solar Power plants?," *Renewable and Sustainable Energy Reviews*, Volume 145, 2021, 111101, https://doi.org/10.1016/j.rser.2021.111101.

[4] For more examples see: Sven Stremke, Dirk Oudes, Paolo Picchi, *The Power of Landscape: Novel Narratives to Engage with the Energy Transition*, (Rotterdam: nai010 publishers, 2022).

[5] See the LAGI 2014 Copenhagen design competition: https://landartgenerator.org.

[6] See the LAGI 2022 Mannheim design competition presented in this book.

Hoover Dam
Photograph courtesy of Sven Stremke

Above: *Energiebaum*
A submission to LAGI 2022 Mannheim by Minu Joshi, Unmesh Lele, Ajay Vaidya, and Minu Joshi. See page 124.

Below: *Energy Duck*
A submission to LAGI 2014 Copenhagen by Hareth Pochee, Adam Khan, Louis Leger, and Patrick Fryer.

concerned tenants may have put up signs suggesting that some sort of permit is needed to enter the grounds. Don't be fooled. Allotment gardens are open to the public and provide many different functions to the greater population. Much like allotment gardens, there are now emerging renewable energy landscapes that welcome the public during daylight hours.[3] Both energy landscapes and garden landscapes can help with rainwater infiltration into groundwater, air quality, leisure possibilities, places to learn about nature, and, above all, beautiful encounters with cultivated nature inside the city.

This multifunctionality presents yet another explanatory variable for the success, popularity, and proliferation of allotment gardens around the world. Allotment gardens provide diverse functions and services for different parts of society. Some are reserved for the actual tenant of the plot, some to the community that runs the allotment garden, and others can be enjoyed by society at large. The allotment garden, in my opinion, presents an excellent model to study equitable distribution of costs and benefits — a prominent topic in present-day social sciences literature on energy transition. While some benefits seem to compensate for the costs (for example, the apples harvested in late summer from the garden tree), other services benefit society at large (in this case the carbon sequestration and positive contribution to the air quality provided by the same apple tree). Can we envision a new type of narrative where solar power plants not only satisfy the economic demands of their owners but also generate functions and services that benefit society at large? What would Moritz Schreber have to say about the benefits to society of our new energy landscapes?

My final question relates to the intrinsic motivations that the great majority of allotment gardeners exhibit. Often (and as witnessed in my own family), these motivations are sustained over generations. What drives people to cultivate and care for land that is in most cases not even owned by them? My personal suspicion, yet to be treated with academic rigor, is that allotment gardens and the activities that take place within their confined spaces improve quality of life for the community at large, and most of all the lives of the gardeners themselves. This possible causal relationship may have significant implications for the way the energy transition should be pursued. Allotment gardeners are neither consumers nor producers, at least not in the conventional macroeconomic understanding of those terms. They are prosumers that exhibit properties of both consumers and producers. Most importantly from a governance perspective is the observation that the limited freedom rendered to the gardeners (to decide what crops to grow when and where) and the physical work that comes with the cultivation of their gardens seem to improve their perceived quality of life.

If we can take these lessons from the Schrebergarten, the transition to renewable energy — beyond its main driver (the mitigation of climate change) — ought to be profitable in economic terms and ought to improve our quality of life. We now have plenty of examples — and more can be seen in the pages of this book — of renewable energy landscapes that are enjoyable and serve useful purposes beyond the production of carbon-free kilowatt-hours. These examples, which improve quality of life, can serve as models for the next few decades of clean energy deployment. This new kind of renewable energy landscape provides contact with natural processes and opportunities to learn about nature. Visitors can play and exercise. Locals gather to engage in social activities amidst the solar panels and meet others visiting their energy gardens.[4] Above all (and more important than we all could have imagined only a few months ago), renewable energy landscapes help to reduce the costs of living and increase self-sufficiency and resilience. It's fascinating that some of the best energy landscapes share all those properties with another type of land use, the invention of which coincided with the previous energy transition and the Industrial Revolution.

If we, the agents of our present energy transition, can foster a common understanding that renewable energy is needed — much like the need for healthy food during industrialization — an important cornerstone for success will be established. The realization of renewable energy projects — similar to the development of allotment gardens — should come with reasonable freedom for those who cultivate the land, allowing for the same kind of democratization of the means of production of energy, along with all of the cultural expression that comes from such freedom. Eventually, and through time, the discourse on renewable energy must be emancipated and liberated from many of the techno-economic considerations that have dominated decision making during the first three decades of this energy transition. And then, perhaps at some stage, we will see miniature working *Energy Ducks*[5] or *Energiebäume*[6] sold in shops around the world — symbols of the pride we share in the transition to renewables that create beautiful places and improve our quality of life.

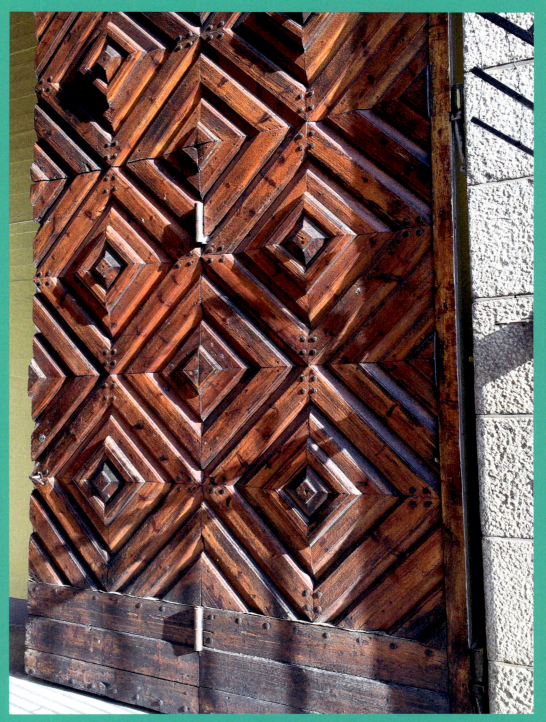

The Solbergfoss hydropower plant. Magnificent woodwork by some unknown but very talented carpenter from southern Norway.
Photograph courtesy of Sven Stremke

Plane of Water
Zsuzsa Péter
See page 56.

"In Germany, today, there exists about 1.4 million allotment gardens. Each gardener can become an active agent making renewable energy beautiful, and some do so already. The 470 square kilometers of German allotment gardens have the potential to not only provide renewable energy to all the families who maintain them, but also to illustrate through experimentation how a changing climate presents a nucleus for socio-technical innovation."

— Sven Stremke
Wageningen University, The Netherlands

SHORTLISTED ENTRIES

Energy Circus
(First Place)

Kaleidoscopic Dune
(Second Place)

HyperSquares

Bloom

Plane of Water

Current Notations

eTREE, an Homage to Nature

Offline Park

H.E.A.R.T.

Yggdrasil

Island of Nature and Art

Unfold

GIRASOLI

Trees and Seesaws

Artee

BAU(M): The Fractal Tree

Bloom: Energy Infrastructure as an Ecosystem Catalyst in a Dry Land

Energiebaum

Energy Generation

Der Bienenstock (The Hive)

Sky Wings

Speak Up

The Barracks: Spinelli Ecological Intersection

The Flourishing Nest

ma duneland

Modular Innovation Cube

Post-Terra

treEcoTopia

Cropergy: Essential Source of Life

Hyperbolic Garden

"Removed from a world in chaos, we take refuge in our gardens. When we place our hands into the earth we connect with the mysteries of the Universe. We ground ourselves in what really matters, with our very sustenance — with cycles of energy; the sun, wind, and water; and with the infinitely complex interrelationships between ecological systems — the nourishment that gives life to human culture."

— Robert Ferry and Elizabeth Monoian
Founding Co-Directors, Land Art Generator Initiative

Energy Circus

DESIGNER: Chai Yi Yang

ENERGY TECHNOLOGY: solar photovoltaic, Vortex Bladeless™ wind turbines, piezoelectric energy harvesting, anaerobic digestion

ANNUAL PRODUCTION: 1,200 MWh

OTHER SOCIAL CO-BENEFITS: pollinator habitat, bird habitat, food production, educational experiences, sustainable waste management, seed bank

What is the ideal relationship between people, landscape, wildlife, energy, and material resources? How can cycles of interconnectedness be demonstrated to the community in a tactile and theatrical experience? What meaning can be found in the future of Spinelli Park?

Energy Circus is a collective ground within which to cultivate intimate relationships between community, landscape, and wildlife through a site-specific shared ecosystem. It offers educational, participatory, and playful experiences, creating an outdoor nave along a primary pedestrian corridor. This leaves the rest of Spinelli Park to grow with natural human activities and organic changes over time.

Energy Circus is designed with an inventory of SEEDs (Socio-Ecological Energizing Devices) to support a holistic ecosystem. These lightweight structures act as a series of energy or resource apparatuses to support four significant domains in the masterplan: civic (fostering collective participation), food (cultivation of productive landscapes), ecology (initiating environmental stewardship), and technology (efficient operation and implementation). Together they create a closed-loop circular system that is observed, celebrated, and learned from by those who explore the park.

On functional display are agrivoltaic fields of solar power and food production, bladeless wind turbines demonstrating new ways of harnessing kinetic energy from the air, piezoelectric films, seed banks, aquaponics, recycling workshops, anaerobic digesters, greenhouses, community kitchens, bioswales, birdhouses, and bee towers.

Energy Circus is a multilayered ecosystem that arises naturally — seeding the park and its surrounding context for a sustainable, resilient, and reciprocal future.

Located within a countryside setting complementing a horticultural theme, the architectural elements of *Energy Circus* recall a cottage typology, constructing an intimate and textured vista at human scale. Primarily made from salvaged industrial materials, the architectural elements of *Energy Circus* are designed for disassembly and adaptation, touching the landscape lightly with low environmental impact.

Energy Circus (continued)

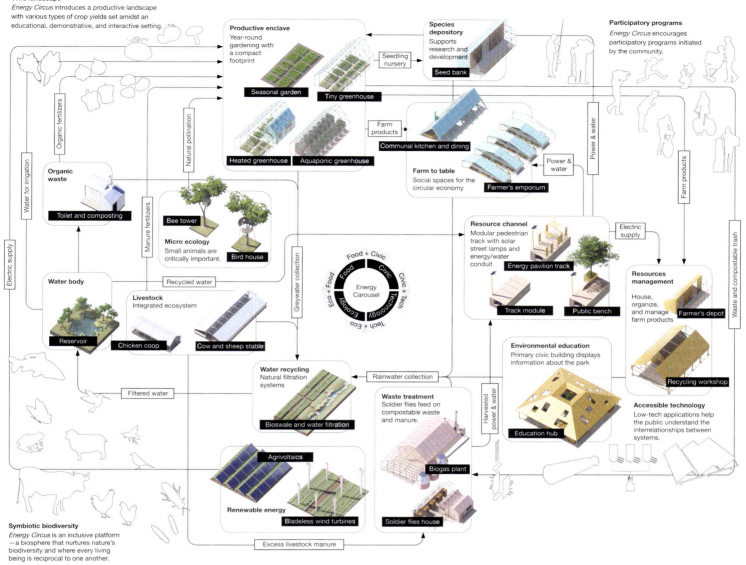
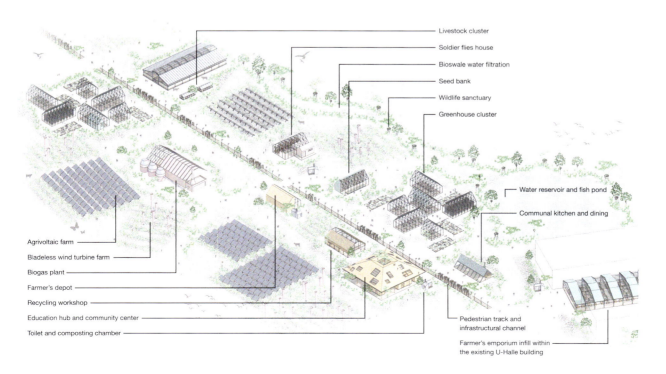

Energy Circus (continued)

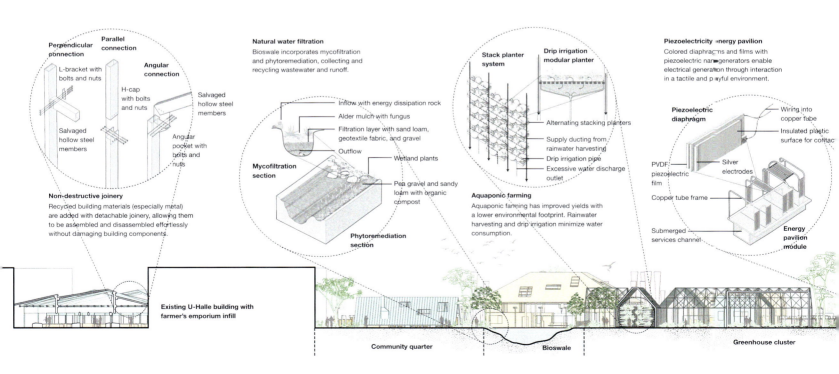

Non-destructive joinery
Recycled building materials (especially metal) are added with detachable joinery, allowing them to be assembled and disassembled effortlessly without damaging building components.

Natural water filtration
Bioswale incorporates mycofiltration and phytoremediation, collecting and recycling wastewater and runoff.

Aquaponic farming
Aquaponic farming has improved yields with a lower environmental footprint. Rainwater harvesting and drip irrigation minimize water consumption.

Piezoelectricity energy pavilion
Colored diaphragms and films with piezoelectric nanogenerators enable electrical generation through interaction in a tactile and playful environment.

54

Integrated with farmlands, the Vortex Bladeless™ wind turbine is suitable in an urban park context.

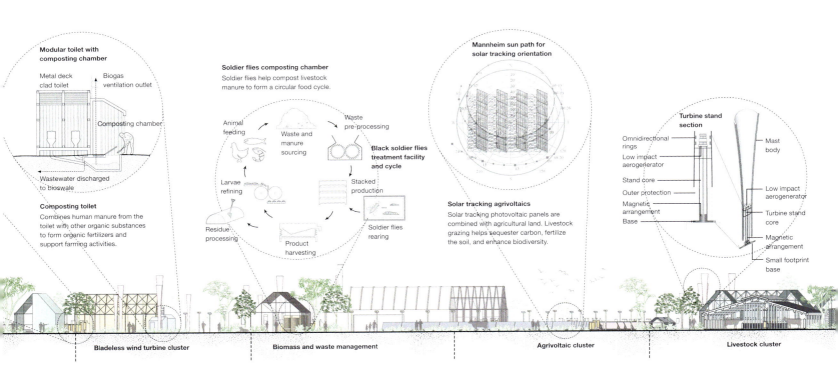

Modular toilet with composting chamber
Metal deck clad toilet
Biogas ventilation outlet
Composting chamber
Wastewater discharged to bioswale

Composting toilet
Combines human manure from the toilet with other organic substances to form organic fertilizers and support farming activities.

Soldier flies composting chamber
Soldier flies help compost livestock manure to form a circular food cycle.

Animal feeding
Waste and manure sourcing
Waste pre-processing
Black soldier flies treatment facility and cycle
Stacked production
Soldier flies rearing
Product harvesting
Residue processing
Larvae refining

Mannheim sun path for solar tracking orientation

Solar tracking agrivoltaics
Solar tracking photovoltaic panels are combined with agricultural land. Livestock grazing helps sequester carbon, fertilize the soil, and enhance biodiversity.

Turbine stand section
Omnidirectional rings
Low impact aerogenerator
Stand core
Outer protection
Magnetic arrangement
Base
Mast body
Low impact aerogenerator
Turbine stand core
Magnetic arrangement
Small footprint base

Bladeless wind turbine cluster | Biomass and waste management | Agrivoltaic cluster | Livestock cluster

Kaleidoscopic Dune

DESIGNERS: Muny-Roth Chev, Jason Daniel, Vatsapol Nanta
ENERGY TECHNOLOGY: concentrator photovoltaics (CPV)
ANNUAL PRODUCTION: 85 MWh
OTHER SOCIAL CO-BENEFITS: public gathering space, food production, playground

Light makes all life on Earth possible and helps define the human experience. *Kaleidoscopic Dune* explores how technology, art, and light merge to define sustainable living in the twenty-first century. Incorporating light as a sculptural and experiential element, the artwork is a modular system of energy generation that is quickly assembled in a variety of forms made from sustainable materials. A system of tensile support masts allows for large open spaces. The flexibility of the structure can accommodate very public functions as well as spaces for private gardens, a playground, and an observatory.

A complete dune system consists of more than 70 repeating hexagonal kaleidoscope modules of reclaimed wood that are coupled in a simple interlocking system. Within each module, colored glass and reflective glass create a kaleidoscope effect for the enjoyment of visitors below. Rising from the center of each kaleidoscope module, a sun-catching cone operates with a dual-axis solar tracking system to align with the position of the sun throughout the day. Each sun-catching cone contains a high performance, multi-junction solar cell that collects the concentrated sunlight from the Fresnel lens at the cone opening and converts it into electricity. A heat sink system keeps the solar cells operating at peak efficiency.

Energy generated by the concentrator photovoltaic modules powers the pavilion, events, and charging areas for personal devices and electric bikes. The remaining energy is sent to the Mannheim city grid. At night, the site glows magically from engineered bioluminescent plants.

At night, visitors to Spinelli Park delight in the kaleidoscopic effects of the LED lighting that is powered entirely by the artwork. Remaining electricity is fed into the grid to power nearby homes.

Kaleidoscopic Dune (continued)

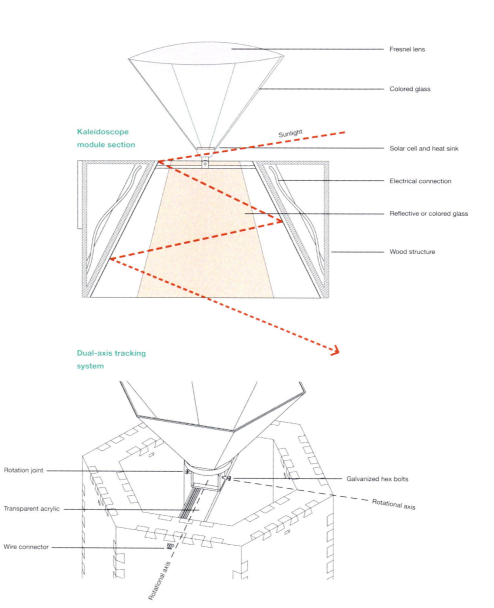

Kaleidoscope module section
- Fresnel lens
- Colored glass
- Sunlight
- Solar cell and heat sink
- Electrical connection
- Reflective or colored glass
- Wood structure

Dual-axis tracking system
- Rotation joint
- Transparent acrylic
- Wire connector
- Galvanized hex bolts
- Rotational axis

A prototype assembly is held up to the sun to illustrate the kaleidoscopic lighting effects of the module.

Axonometric site plan

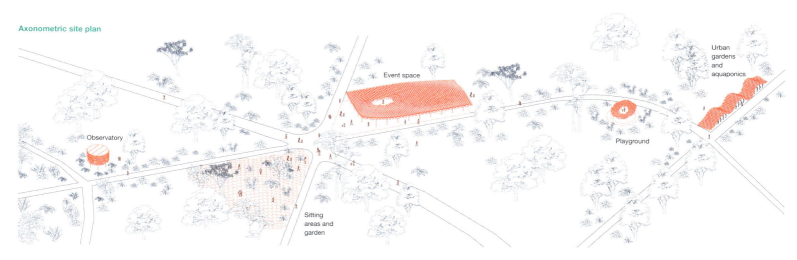

- Observatory
- Sitting areas and garden
- Event space
- Playground
- Urban gardens and aquaponics

58

As the sun sets, the lighting effects of the artwork shift from being generated by refracted sunlight to being generated by programmable LED lights.

HyperSquares

DESIGNERS: Zilan Wang, Ziting Wang

ENERGY TECHNOLOGY: solar photovoltaic, micro vertical axis wind turbines, microbial fuel cells (MFC), kinetic energy harvesting

ANNUAL PRODUCTION: 6,500 MWh

OTHER SOCIAL CO-BENEFITS: community greenhouse, playground, electronic device charging

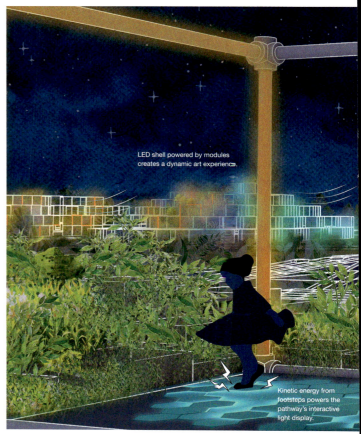

Kinetic energy pop-up

Nicknamed "Quadratestadt," the City of Mannheim is built in a grid pattern, making it unique among other German cities. Paying homage to the city's "square" history and inspired by the natural geological features of the site, *HyperSquares* imagines Mannheim's post-carbon future with a cluster of installations that emerge from the landscape in the form of dunes of stacked cubes. The design reflects the intersections between Mannheim's past and future, nature and culture, art and technology, and explores topics related to climate change, green energy, and urban farming.

Eschewing homogenized large-scale energy harvesting machines, *HyperSquares* redefines the energy production landscape, allowing for playful, dynamic, interactive programmed spaces using diverse combinations of modular forms that provide scalable solutions. The three-meter cube *HyperSquares* modules include three types of components: faces, frame and joint, and add-ons. Faces integrate green technologies to harvest renewable energy, which are connected by frame and joint components with internal circuits for transporting electricity. The frame is wrapped with an LED shell that produces different lighting effects in response to the collected energy harvest data. Finally, add-on programs cater to the needs of different groups of people.

HyperSquares integrates solar, wind, microbial fuel cell, and kinetic energy harvesting technologies to provide energy with multiple social co-benefits on both civic and residential scales. Three-dimensional multifunctional spaces offer interactive play and performance, planted terraces, greenhouses, and biodiverse habitats, reflecting three major themes of art and culture, nature and water, and play and education. Visitors to Spinelli Park will have an opportunity to visit and interact with a portion of this energy landscape, learn about how the systems function, and reserve a spot for their very own plug-in module for backyards or kleingärten.

HyperSquares enriches people's lives socially, recreationally, and educationally, confirming the city's slogan that life is lived to the fullest when it is "squared."

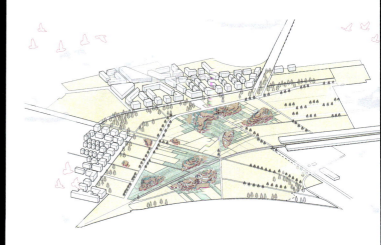

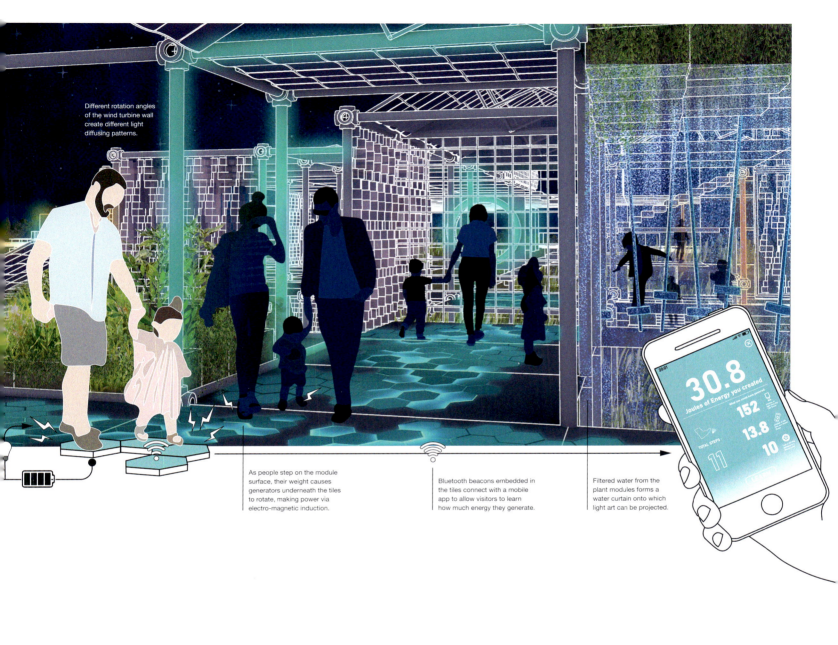

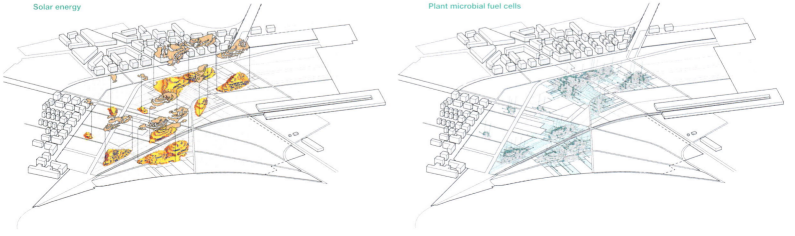

HyperSquares (continued)

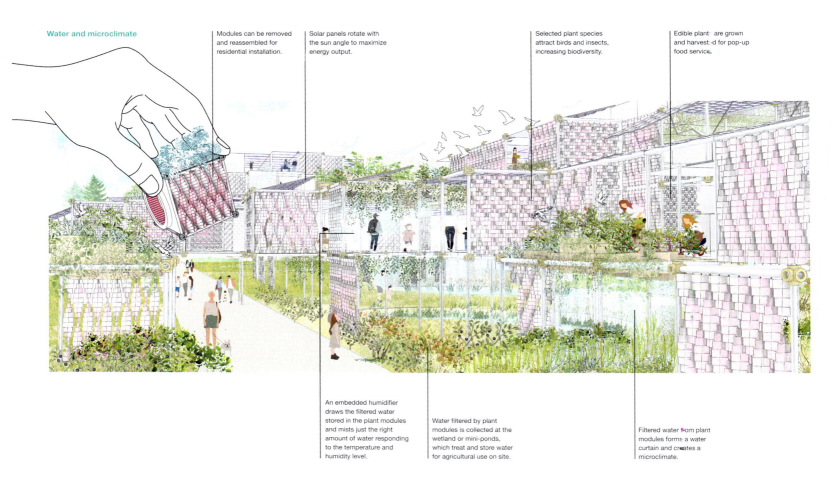

Water and microclimate

Modules can be removed and reassembled for residential installation.

Solar panels rotate with the sun angle to maximize energy output.

Selected plant species attract birds and insects, increasing biodiversity.

Edible plants are grown and harvested for pop-up food service.

An embedded humidifier draws the filtered water stored in the plant modules and mists just the right amount of water responding to the temperature and humidity level.

Water filtered by plant modules is collected at the wetland or mini-ponds, which treat and store water for agricultural use on site.

Filtered water from plant modules forms a water curtain and creates a microclimate.

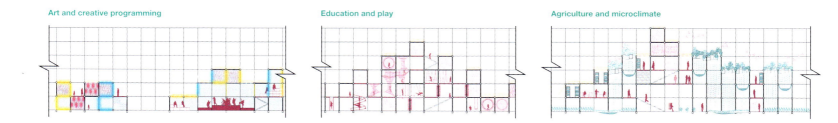

Art and creative programming

Education and play

Agriculture and microclimate

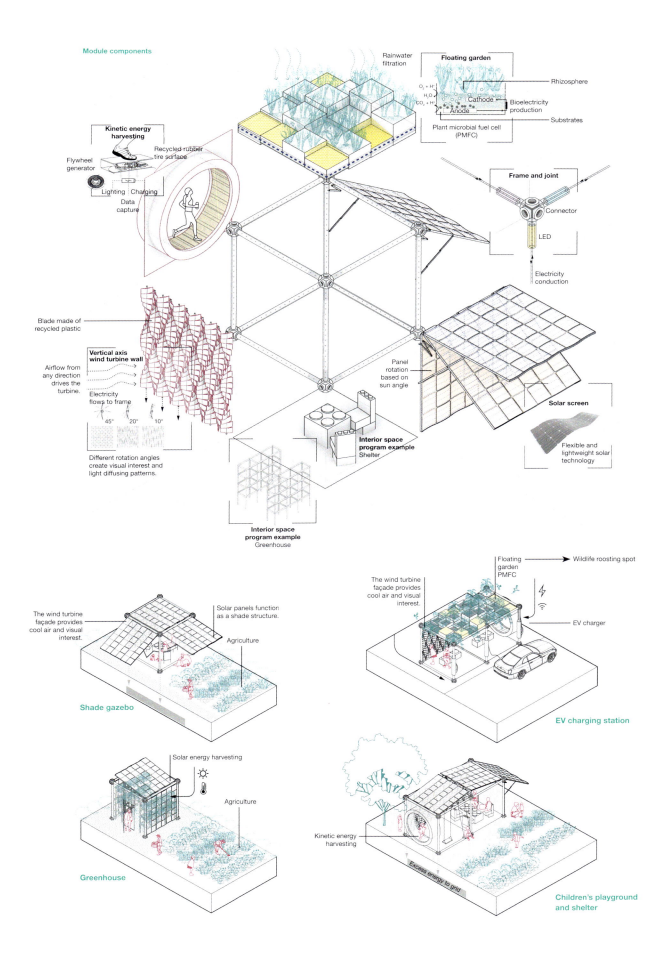

Bloom

DESIGNERS: Mateusz Góra, Agata Gryszkiewicz
ENERGY TECHNOLOGY: solar photovoltaic
ANNUAL PRODUCTION: 5 MWh per module (45 MWh for a 9-module array or 125 MWh for a 25-module array)
OTHER SOCIAL CO-BENEFITS: public gathering space, food production, rainwater harvesting, public marketplace

Bloom **is a power generating,** adaptable art installation that is inspired by nastic movements in plants — the opening and closing of blossoms and leaves in response to stimuli, such as sunlight. Similar to the petals of flowers, *Bloom* adapts and transforms itself according to daylight, the seasons, and natural cycles.

The tilt of the solar panels adjusts according to the sun's position to generate the optimum amount of clean energy, while changing the way each *Bloom* module relates to the public.

This dynamic movement creates an element of surprise for visitors to Spinelli Park, revealing hidden, inner public spaces that appear different with each visit. The shaded outdoor "rooms" are made from sustainably sourced wood and fitted with various social functions ranging from lounging area to market stand, mini cafe, bicycle repair shop, or play area. The plants growing in and around *Bloom* purify the air and create an atmosphere of a hidden winter garden.

When closing during the night or in colder seasons, *Bloom* provides protection from the elements. Compact greenhouses located in the upper modules are visible from the outside — a symbol of the importance of sustainable and space-efficient agriculture. The greenhouses produce tomatoes, lettuce, spinach, onion, cabbage, peppers, lettuce, chard, cabbage, arugula, kale, and collard greens.

Bloom works across scales. One module can be installed in a private garden, or multiple modules can come together to create complex "pattern clusters" that grow fractally. These fractal patterns have a number of advantages. They create larger, shaded, and protected outdoor public spaces with grids of open "pockets" of green space. At large enough aggregations, they begin to function as utility-scale infrastructure that increases public well-being.

The solar panels located on the four walls of each *Bloom* module can provide up to 5 MWh of clean energy per year, more than enough for an efficient, single-family home or an allotment garden. A rainwater collection system can provide up to 400 liters of water for use in each greenhouse.

Visitors to Spinelli Park in the summer months will find the solar panels tilted into their most open position, reaching for the sun like flowers or plant leaves reach for the optimum amount of sunlight.

Nourished by rainwater drip irrigation and dappled sunlight, urban vegetable gardens grow in greenhouse lofts above gathering places, reading nooks, eating areas, and market stands.

Bloom (continued)

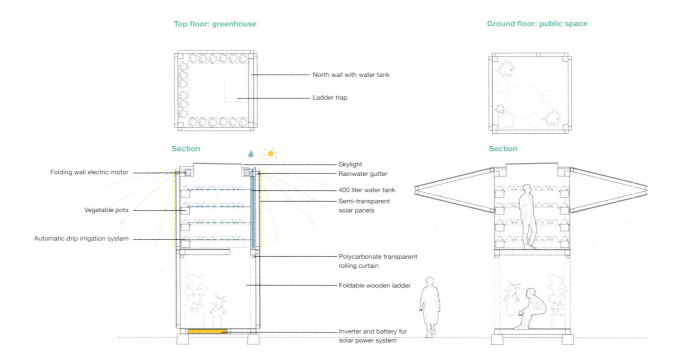

The outer layer of *Bloom* adapts by opening and closing following the sun conditions. During the night or cold seasons it closes entirely to protect plants and public space inside.

A nine-module installation seen from above in the summertime.

Fractal patterns
Modularity allows for fractal-like growth and flexibility. Patterns can be deployed based on desired density, the relationships between public spaces, and the program of social functions.

    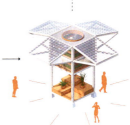

Modularity
Prefab, modular, wooden structure with low impact foundations

Dualism
Double social function: agriculture and public space/winter garden

Tradition
Outer wall structure as a reference to the pattern of traditional German timber wall technology

Protection
Recyclable polycarbonate protection for outside walls and inner layer for thermal protection and partial transparency

Energy
Semi-transparent solar cells on the upper module generate clean energy and allow sunlight to pass through.

Mystery
Closed structure creates an atmosphere of mystery and curiosity about what is hidden inside each module.

Adaptability
Walls fold to adapt the solar panel tilt to the best possible sun angle while revealing public space below.

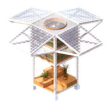  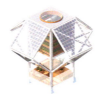

Summer
Tilt angle from 15–35 degrees
Public space open during the day and closed at night
Greenhouse operational

Spring
Tilt angle from 35–50 degrees
Public space open during the day and closed at night
Greenhouse operational

Autumn
Tilt angle from 50–65 degrees
Public space closed
Inner polycarbon curtain
Greenhouse operational

Winter
Tilt angle from 65–75 degrees
Public space closed
Inner polycarbon curtain
Greenhouse operational

Night
Tilt angle 90 degrees
Public space closed
Greenhouse operational

Townhouse backyard
Bloom scaled for a backyard could generate clean energy that will meet most of the household energy demand plus serve as a garden pavilion that could be personalized for color and function.

Schrebergärten
Bloom installations in Schrebergärten could be private or shared by multiple owners. They can be personalized in terms of function and color and could supply power for garden plots, store energy, or sell it to the grid.

Park or square
Bloom installations in a larger public spaces could stand alone or create a landscape of interactive patterns, where public spaces relate to one another.

Plane of Water

DESIGNER: Zsuzsa Péter
ENERGY TECHNOLOGY: organic photovoltaic (OPV) solar
ANNUAL PRODUCTION: 40 MWh
OTHER SOCIAL CO-BENEFITS: shaded public space, water harvesting, urban garden

An undulating, shimmering, translucent surface stretches across a segment of Spinelli Park. From a distance it appears as a floating *Plane of Water* above a thriving garden, creating a peaceful space for reflection in the heart of the city. The large outdoor artwork is a glimpse into the future of energy and agriculture and their collaboration within the field of agrivoltaics.

Tensioned, lightweight, hyperbolic surfaces woven with silvery translucent organic photovoltaic (OPV) solar film create a space of shade, shelter, and gathering for park visitors under the glimmering canopy. The translucency allows vegetation to grow underneath, protected from the more harmful spectrum of the sun's rays. Some of the electricity generated by the canopy is used to pump harvested water into an elevated tank—an organizing sculptural element that supplies the gravity-fed drip irrigation system.

Plane of Water is able to provide irrigation water for nearly three hectares of the park while giving back to the city a majority of the clean electricity generated.

Smaller versions of the artwork, suitable for residential use, consist of a fragment of the structure coupled with a smaller elevated water tank of one cubic meter capacity. They function by the same principle, aiding the growth of decorative plants or vegetables underneath a solar canopy. The canopies can be closed on all sides, becoming greenhouses as are often found in the Schrebergärten of Mannheim.

Light connections to the ground along with the translucency and porosity of the canopy mean that *Plane of Water* has a minimal impact on existing ecosystems, allowing the ecology of the park to flourish underneath.

Plane of Water provides sufficient irrigation to maintain nearly three hectares of the Spinelli Park landscape while also supplying clean electricity to surrounding households.

The tensile support structure is deceptively strong, capable of withstanding high winds in spite of the ephemeral and gossimer aesthetic of the installation.

Plane of Water (continued)

The light grey dye of the organic photovoltaic material is engineered to appear almost white and blend in with an overcast sky. Organic photovoltaic technology is capable of generating consistent amounts of electricity in lower light level conditions. As visitors move through the artwork the rippling geometries separate into greys and overlap into whites in a dynamic interplay of soft light and softer shadow.

Plane of Water (continued)

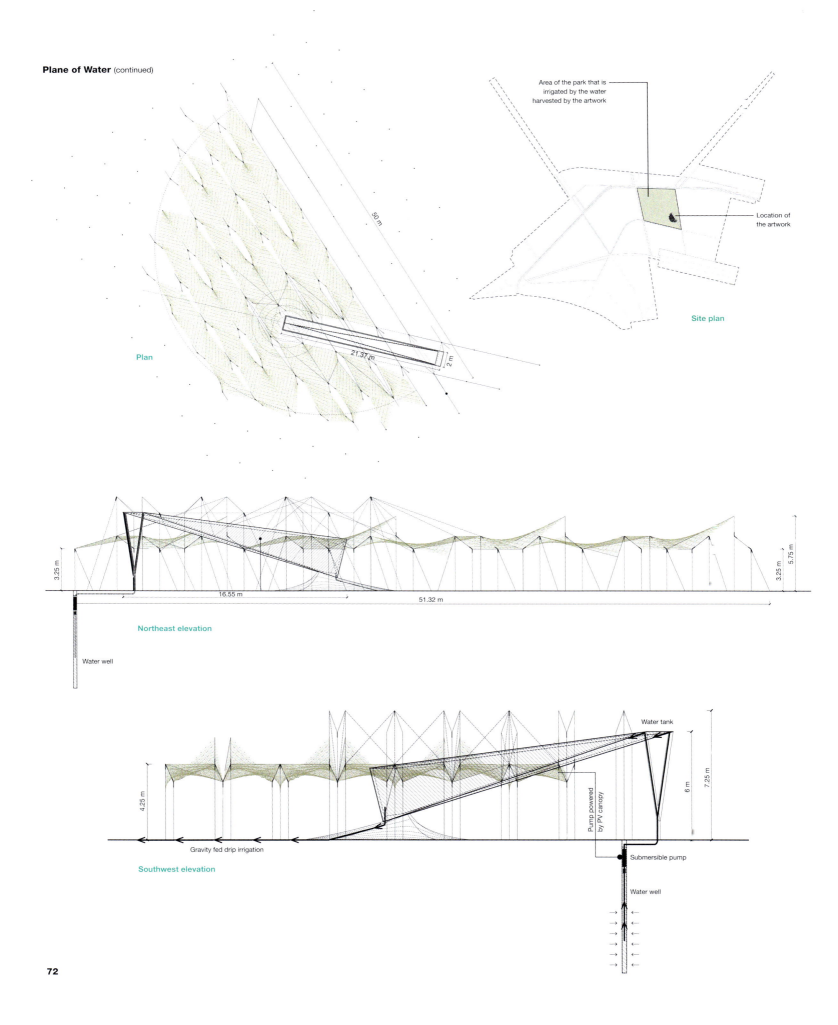

Two small units generate electricity and harvest water for growing vegetables in a German kleingarten. One opens to the air and one has closed sides to act as a greenhouse.

Current Notations

DESIGNERS: Jonathan Craig, Lucas Denit
ENERGY TECHNOLOGY: solar photovoltaic, battery energy storage
ANNUAL PRODUCTION: 582 MWh
OTHER SOCIAL CO-BENEFITS: temperate microclimates, stormwater collection and treatment

Mannheim is a city born from water. For millennia, the Rhine and Neckar rivers carved a meandering course across the Rhine Plain. Historically, these habitats existed in a state of symbiotic balance with the flooding of the river. As Mannheim developed, their courses were channelized according to the efficient and linear logic of commerce and exchange. The ecosystems, which for so many millennia maintained a delicate system balance, were thrown out of order. Today, climate change is altering precipitation patterns across the globe. Alpine rivers are running dangerously low due to uncertain snowfall and infrequent summer rain. In 2022, Europe was rocked by previously unknown heat, extended droughts, and crop yield losses, while the great ancient rivers of the Loire, Po, Danube, and Rhine began to run dry.

Current Notations adapts the reclaimed Spinelli Barracks as a site of hybrid ecologies, reconfiguring the synthetic material of the barracks into new formations that recall the contours of the primordial landscape of the floodplain. Through a syntax of berms (earthwork embankments from the salvaged concrete of the old barracks), fins (linear photovoltaic arrays), and totems (battery storage towers) at four key cyclist and pedestrian intersections, *Current Notations* gently lifts the meadow and inscribes a pattern of channels and berms that funnel stormwater into concealed cisterns for storage and redistribution. As the berms trace, hug, and pull away from the walkways in a dreamlike recollection of the watercourses that once flowed freely through the meadow, they offer shade, respite, evaporative cooling effects, and a sense of wonder to those passing between their banks. The native meadow species within the long slope of the berm contrast with the ferns and mosses that thrive in the shadier, cooler, and wetter biomes of tree-lined riverbanks.

The abstracted riverbed landscape conceals a technical program of water collection, retention, and distribution enabled by on-site electricity generation. A photovoltaic array perches on the crest of the berm, rising like the dorsal fin of a great fish. Panels are positioned to optimize electrical production and to shade the pedestrian channel below. Misters are concealed within panels on the back face of the photovoltaic arrays. Slim steel arms and tension cabling stand in visual juxtaposition to the heavy geologic features of the berm. Punctuating the field condition of berms and fins is a family of totems dotting the meadow. Their unassuming presence conceals the battery packs, distribution equipment, and control systems mounted on vertical racks inside.

Walking within the earth berm pathways, visitors to Spinelli Park will experience a significant drop in temperature and an increase in relative humidity within the microclimate created by the artwork.

Current Notations (continued)

Totems are activated as landscape markers with integrated lights.

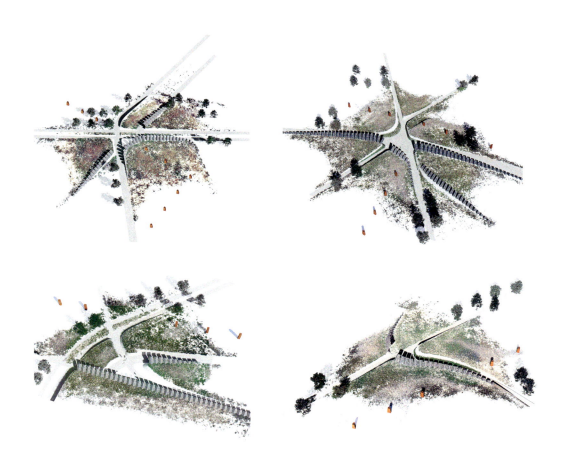

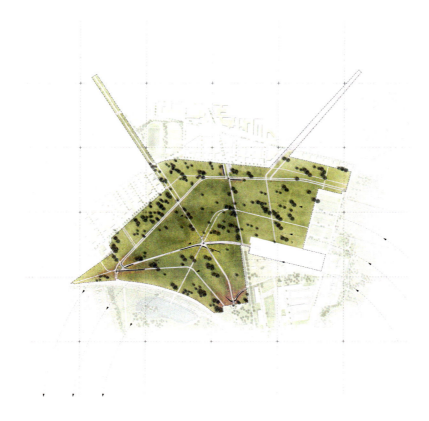

Four sites form a connective network of microclimate interventions across the new park. A landscape funnels stormwater to concealed cisterns for storage and distribution. The sum effect of the installation is one of deep experience — of walking through a new landscape simultaneously artificial and intensely native. *Current Notations* distills the many lives of the landscape into a coherent whole.

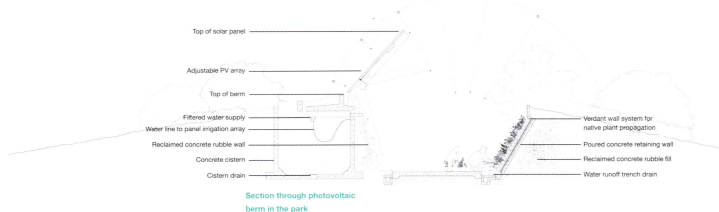

Section through photovoltaic berm in the park

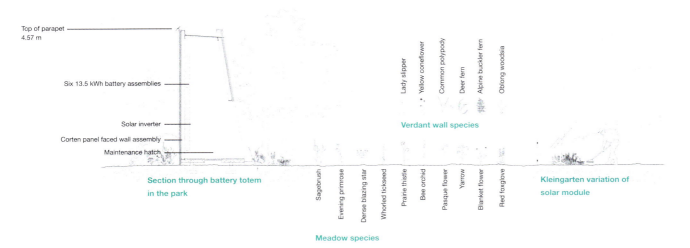

Section through battery totem in the park

Meadow species

Verdant wall species

Kleingarten variation of solar module

eTREE, an Homage to Nature

DESIGNERS: Joo Hyung Oh, Jaeho Yoon, Yechan Shin, Suin Kim, Sunjae Yu, Jinhyeok Ryu, Sooyoung Cho
ENERGY TECHNOLOGY: thin-film solar photovoltaic, kinetic energy harvesting
ANNUAL PRODUCTION: 6,500 MWh
OTHER SOCIAL CO-BENEFITS: personal device charging, shaded gathering space

Nature has already perfected the art of sustainable energy generation in the form of trees. Beautiful in aesthetics and function, trees generate the energy that they need to survive while providing other forms of life with oxygen, shade, and nutrients. *eTREE* emulates this positive natural cycle by harnessing the powers of the sun and the wind to generate clean energy.

The membrane of *eTREE*—an abstraction of tree leaves—is 3D printed from recycled wood cellulose filament. This fibrous material is lightweight and durable, and can withstand a large amount of tensile stress. Similar to the way that leaves on a tree produce energy through photosynthesis, *eTREE* produces energy with solar cells that are scattered along the fabric membrane. The distribution of the solar cells is optimized by the path of the sun around the installation much like a tree grows to maximize its own solar energy collection.

The frame of *eTREE* represents the branches and is pre-tensioned to withstand sagging due to gravity and to counter lateral wind loads. The rigid frame and the fibrous membrane counteract each other's forces in a sturdy equilibrium, much like in a pop-up tent.

The central trunk of *eTREE* supports the membrane and frame, which are free to oscillate up and down as wind flows from any direction. Generators are distributed along the trunk to convert the kinetic energy of this oscillation into additional electricity.

The batteries buried in the ground below *eTREE* represent the roots of the tree. Just like plants store nutrients in their roots, *eTREE* stores electrical energy in these battery cells. This stored energy is used to power electric bicycles and other electronic devices for visitors to Spinelli Park. The remaining energy is sent to the power grid of the City of Mannheim.

The lightweight, modular nature of *eTREE* allows it to be assembled, disassembled, flattened, and moved with ease. The *eTREE* designed for Mannheim has a total of six revolutions in the spiral and measures 15 meters in height with a diameter of 14 meters. Other variations can be made to fit sites of various scales.

eTREE emulates the regenerative cycles of trees by harnessing the power of the sun and the wind to create clean energy.

Visitors can use the power outlets connected to *eTREE* to charge their electric bicycles and their personal devices. Sensors gather data on weather and energy consumption and display real-time information to the public through interactive displays. Most of the energy is left to flow into the city grid. Eventually, *eTREE* artworks begin to pop up all over town, from office parks to kleingärten.

eTREE, an Homage to Nature (continued)

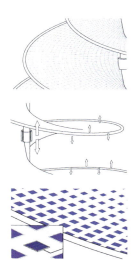

The frame of *eTREE* is pre-tensioned to withstand sagging due to gravity. The GRP (glass fiber reinforced plastic) and the membrane counteract each other's forces in a sturdy equilibrium.

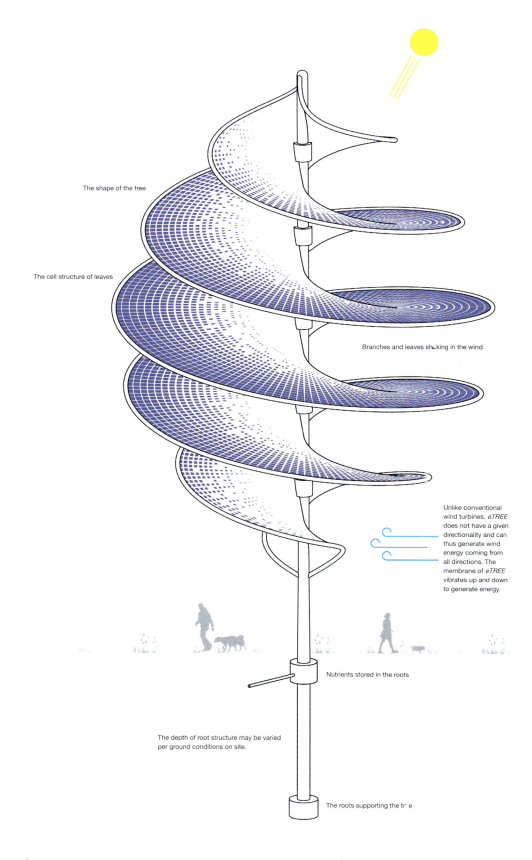

The shape of the tree

The cell structure of leaves

Branches and leaves shaking in the wind

Unlike conventional wind turbines, *eTREE* does not have a given directionality and can thus generate wind energy coming from all directions. The membrane of *eTREE* vibrates up and down to generate energy.

Nutrients stored in the roots

The depth of root structure may be varied per ground conditions on site.

The roots supporting the tree

Process on site
1. The modular system allows *eTREE* to be transported with a much smaller footprint than when it is assembled.
2. The precast concrete pile foundation is installed.
3. The stem of *eTREE* is erected.
4. The frame of the membrane is installed at the topmost point of *eTREE*.
5. The membrane is fed through the frame. Gravity and tensile forces allow the structure to be in equilibrium without the need for extra substructures.
6. *eTREEs* blending into their natural settings.
7. *eTREE* being disassembled in reverse order.
8. The unfolded membrane is folded again.
9. Disassembled *eTREE* is moved to a new location.

eTREE is an excellent wayfinding device. Allées help guide people along a path to groupings that create outdoor rooms in the park.

The spiral form of *eTREE* as seen from above, its canopy

Offline Park

DESIGNERS: David Vardy, Jiayi Xu, Yuzhang Su, Jinyu Li, Xuanrun Yi, Evan Saarinen

ENERGY TECHNOLOGY: spherical solar photovoltaic (similar to Sphelar™), microbial fuel cells (MFC)

ANNUAL PRODUCTION: 3,085 MWh

OTHER SOCIAL CO-BENEFITS: food production, carbon sequestration, public space free from electromagnetic radiation

The German Schrebergarten was the late nineteenth century garden-as-antidote prescription to the rapid growth of the industrial city — a green escape for mental well-being among the suffocation of the metropolis. Today, our health is no longer threatened primarily by the industrial city, but rather by the new culture of data overabundance and our inability to switch-off. The park of the twenty-first century will therefore be an *Offline Park* — an urban space shielding electromagnetic radiation — freeing visitors from the suffocation of an always-alert life.

Offline Park is an energy landscape that provides clean power to the city and places the power consumption of personal devices on pause. The solar canopy that defines the artwork is a woven 96% open mesh incorporating a multitude of micro-spherical solar cells. It also acts like a Faraday cage to form a healthy shield against electromagnetic radiation. This protection from electromagnetic frequencies (EMF) may also protect butterflies and other insects and serves as a field of study on the impacts of EMF on pollinator biodiversity.

Micro-spherical solar is able to generate electricity while receiving the sun's rays from nearly any direction. It can therefore be incorporated into an undulating surface, such as that formed by a mesh or textile.

The reforestation of the former Spinelli Barracks contributes carbon sequestration, flora and fauna habitat, and the mitigation of the heat island effect. Plant microbial fuel cells utilize areas of healthy soils within the forest for energy generation and wastewater purification.

The *Offline Park* solar canopy is supported by a living willow structure rather than by an energy-intensive concrete and steel structure. Its form is inspired by the art nouveau light stands of the Wasserturm (water tower) in Mannheim. The site plan is laid out as a palimpsest memorial tracing of the site history and producing a ghosted synthesis of previous structures and cultivations.

The canopy powers and protects multi-purpose platforms and courtyards that change over time through the interaction of people with the root balls of the willows and by opening and closing sections of canopy to create new microclimates and greenhouse effects.

The canopy powers and protects multi-purpose platforms and courtyards that change over time through the interaction of people with the root balls of the willows. Sections of canopy can be opened and closed to create new microclimates and greenhouse effects.

Offline Park (continued)

Visitors to Spinelli Park enjoy a spring day in an outdoor cafe. Undistracted by electronic devices, they are free to have deep and focused conversations with friends and perhaps are open to new encounters.

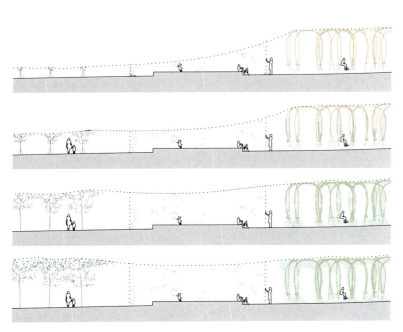

As the willows start to grow, they lift up the mesh and create more space within the park over time.

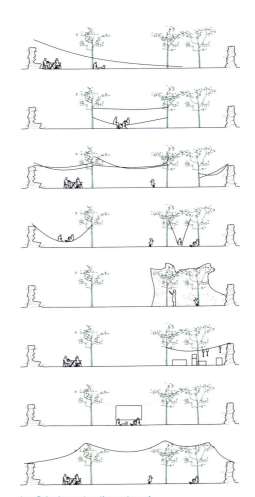

In a Schrebergarten, the system of micro-spherical solar mesh textile is tied between trees and connected to fences to cover willow sculptures. The possibilities are as varied as the Schrebergärten themselves.

Families visiting *Offline Park* can play, picnic, chat, exercise, and rediscover nature, all free from the potential distractions of the outside world. Within this park, time seems almost to stand still and the sounds of nature can clearly be heard.

85

H.E.A.R.T.

DESIGNERS: Mariano Quiroga Robles, Milagros Aguilar Plaza (HABITÁCULO)

ENERGY TECHNOLOGY: flexible thin-film solar photovoltaic

ANNUAL PRODUCTION: 650 MWh

OTHER SOCIAL CO-BENEFITS: landscape irrigation, shaded gathering space

The namesake of Spinelli Park — the former Spinelli Barracks that was returned to the City of Mannheim in 2013 — is U.S. Private First Class Dominic V. Spinelli. A medic at age 21, he was mortally wounded near the village of Wilsbach on April 14, 1945 as he attempted to rescue four wounded comrades.

At the center of the new park that carries Spinelli's name, *H.E.A.R.T.* celebrates the selfless actions of one man and calls on all of us to give of ourselves for the benefit of others. The heart of Spinelli Park is also the heart of Mannheim. It is a space to celebrate love for our planet.

This *Holistic Engine for Adaptive and Restorative Transformation* also recalls the ancient and winding channels of the Neckar River, reminding us that the river gives life to the landscape, and the river gave form to the city.

Through a network of vein-like canals that reach out into the surrounding city, *H.E.A.R.T.* collects stormwater and treats it using part of the energy generated from the sculptural solar canopy at the heart of the installation. The treated water is used to give life to a nursery garden nestled within mounded landforms created from the earth and stones at the site.

Nature breaks through and emerges in the form of trees and plants that coexist with sustainable technologies that mimic the natural process of photosynthesis. The clean electricity generated by the artwork is used to pump water through filtration and irrigation systems and to light the park. The remainder is supplied to the community via the city grid.

As the wind flows into the city by way of the Rhine-Neckar Climate Corridor, it causes a periodic change in air pressure below the solar canopy, generating a subtle movement of the diaphragm that from a distance appears almost like the beating of a heart.

This regenerative gesture in the landscape serves as a public and educational space for all ages and supports the programs of the nearby Bertha Hirsch School. It is a gathering place and productive landscape for all the people of Mannheim.

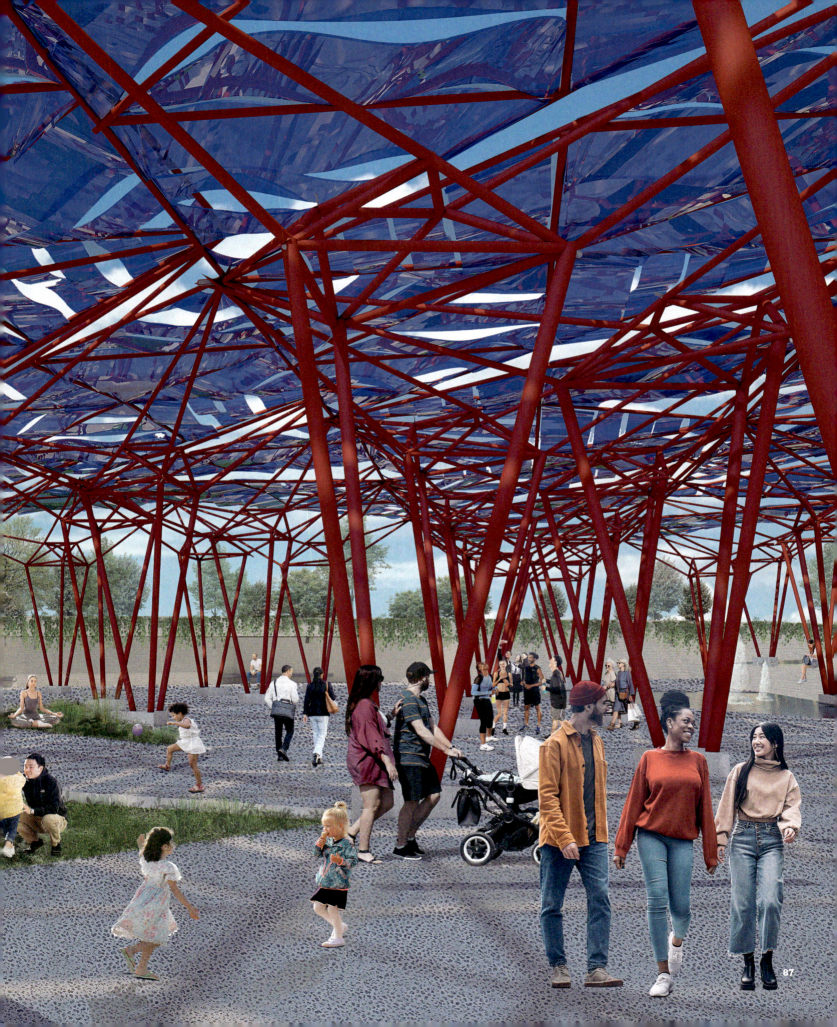

H.E.A.R.T. (continued)

Site plan

1. Völklinger Str. axis
2. St. Hildegard and Philippuskirche
3. Bertha Hirsch School
4. U-Halle
5. Connection to lake in natural reserved area (Old Neckar River route)

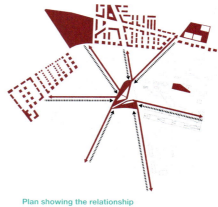

Plan showing the relationship between *H.E.A.R.T.* and the surrounding housing, educational, and civic areas.

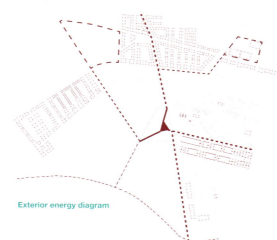

Exterior energy diagram

Exterior water route diagram

Interior water route diagram

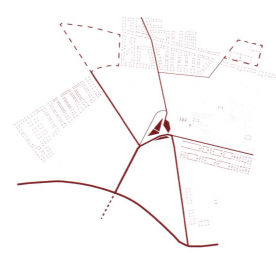

88

Nursery garden platforms

Yggdrasil

DESIGNERS: Cheung Man Kit, Solomon Cheung, Lai Ho Yin, Julio Lai
ENERGY TECHNOLOGY: solar photovoltaic, kinetic energy paving
ANNUAL PRODUCTION: 120 MWh
OTHER SOCIAL CO-BENEFITS: wayfinding, time measure

What is the definition of natural beauty? Is it possible to reflect a kind of natural beauty through the innovation of new technologies? *Yggdrasil* — named after the immense sacred tree in Germanic mythology — explores the art of eidonomy (the study of the external appearance of an organism) as applied to mechanical forms. The artwork mimics the beauty of dynamic natural morphologies while functioning as a clock tower in Spinelli Park.

Clock towers were first erected at fairs during the Industrial Age in the late nineteenth century. A source of rivalries between nations, clock making was once a symbol of artistic and horological excellence and holds important significance in human history.

Carrying this tradition forward, *Yggdrasil* sits at the crossroads of the park and celebrates a new era of technology. It is a power generator that also presents a new interpretation of renewable energy technologies. The form is inspired from the anatomy of plants and the morphological variations of their diurnal and life cycles, a metaphor for the flow of time throughout a day.

An integrated mechanical system at the core, much like a hinged stem, causes the artwork to slowly expand and contract from day to night. Located on top of the column, a clock hand connects to the motor inside the column which translates movement to the folding skeleton.

The mechanism is enveloped by a number of triangular photovoltaic solar modules, or petals, to form the changing shape of *Yggdrasil*.

The artwork is fabricated from local recycled scrap steel that is manufactured using electric arc furnace (EAF) production to minimize emissions by 80%. The body is composed of six stacking levels of radial skeleton. Each level consists of two layers of diamond-shaped, movable structure. Inside are a series of identical steel members with hinge joints on both ends. Eight modules connect the outer layer to the column, allowing linear movement while transferring wind load to the column.

Surrounding *Yggdrasil* is a 20-meter diameter circular plaza covered by triangular floor tiles with embedded kinetic energy generators. As visitors walk around the tower to check the time, they generate additional electricity through these tiles. The automated movement and lighting take only a small percentage of the energy generated by the artwork. The rest is used to power the surrounding park.

As the sky gradually loses daylight, *Yggdrasil* returns to its folded form and LED lighting begins to glow inside the tower core. The soft light spilling from the gaps within the façade creates a vertical lantern for wayfinding and a poetic moment for those who linger on their way.

Yggdrasil is inspired by the history of clocks and their intricate function. The form expresses a fascination with craftsmanship for our new age of post-industrialization and artificial intelligence.

Yggdrasil (continued)

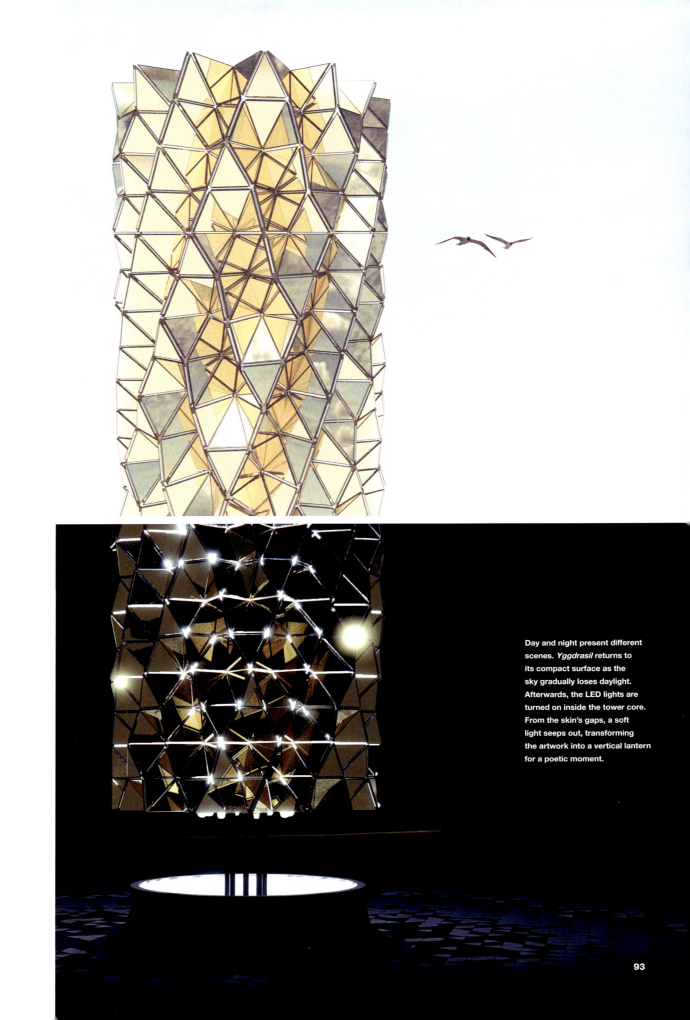

Day and night present different scenes. *Yggdrasil* returns to its compact surface as the sky gradually loses daylight. Afterwards, the LED lights are turned on inside the tower core. From the skin's gaps, a soft light seeps out, transforming the artwork into a vertical lantern for a poetic moment.

Yggdrasil (continued)

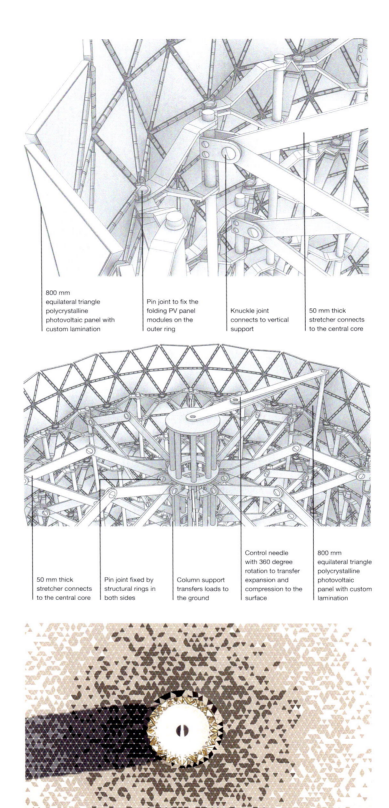

| 800 mm equilateral triangle polycrystalline photovoltaic panel with custom lamination | Pin joint to fix the folding PV panel modules on the outer ring | Knuckle joint connects to vertical support | 50 mm thick stretcher connects to the central core |

| 50 mm thick stretcher connects to the central core | Pin joint fixed by structural rings in both sides | Column support transfers loads to the ground | Control needle with 360 degree rotation to transfer expansion and compression to the surface | 800 mm equilateral triangle polycrystalline photovoltaic panel with custom lamination |

Aerial view of *Yggdrasil* showing the gradual change in color of the surrounding kinetic energy pavers that repeat the triangular pattern of the tower.

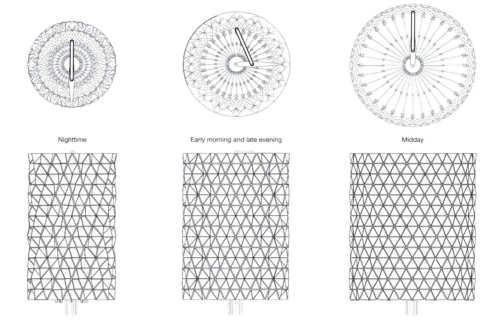

Time indication by change of form

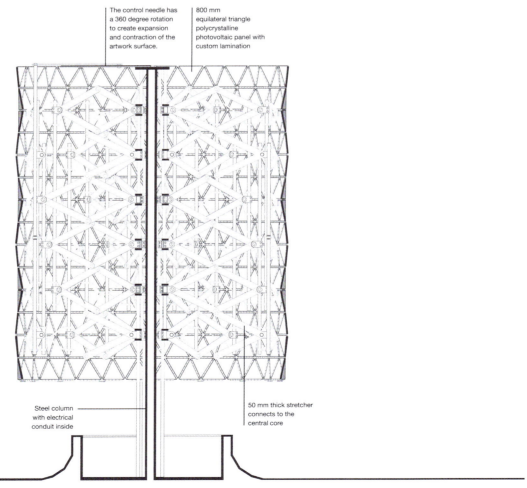

Section diagram

Island of Nature and Art

DESIGNERS: Bartosz Haduch, Bartlomiej Bogucki, Łukasz Marjanski (NArchitekTURA)

ENERGY TECHNOLOGY: perovskite solar photovoltaic tile

ANNUAL PRODUCTION: 582 MWh

OTHER SOCIAL CO-BENEFITS: public gathering space, mobile and interactive play and performance venues, stormwater collection

Island of Nature and Art is a public city square and an enclave of contemplation. The artwork supports a thriving social ecosystem that in turn supports the natural ecosystem while reinforcing the paths and viewsheds of this contemporary park.

The project includes several different spatial interventions that can be implemented in stages. The central part of the proposal is a kind of anti-square, the form of which is clad in perovskite solar photovoltaic tiles. The square is not entirely flat (or square). Instead, its gentle slopes create places for rest and recreation, and are surrounded by water and dense local greenery. Its irregular form organically extends the realm of pedestrian traffic. The raised corners emphasize the most important viewing axes, making the *Island* visible from further perspectives and giving it the character of an intimate urban interior.

Access to this part of the park is accentuated by three large openings in the bent corners of the square. These elements act as "gates" to the central square. The arch provides a proscenium frame for outdoor events, such as exhibitions and performances.

The main part of the square is surrounded by a shallow body of water. The reservoir is bedded with white aggregate and forms a rain garden, which can also be used to store and redistribute rainwater. It is designed to be beautiful when dry, hosting a diverse ecosystem of native riparian plants.

The existing tracks from the U-Halle building provide a dynamic platform for mobile wagons with places for rest, relaxation, play, and ever-changing performances. Extending out from the central square, lavender fields merge with delicate photovoltaic lamps that move in the wind. Japanese maple trees mix with glowing solar PV umbrellas in the shape of various scaled "hats." Cherry and plum trees surround benches made of reflective material that emit a soft underglow at night as bioluminescent aggregate causes the lines of the pathways to glow softly, extending out to the city in different directions.

Multifunctional trolleys are built on the existing old train tracks of Spinelli.

Island of Nature and Art (continued)

The square is an island dedicated to nature, art, and ecology surrounded by a shallow body of water. The artwork recedes into the background amidst the surrounding sea of flowers, greenery, and the water's reflections.

Unfold

DESIGNERS: Zicheng Zhao, Priyanjali Sinha, Andreina Sojo, Menghan Yu, Wei Xia

ENERGY TECHNOLOGY: organic photovoltaic (OPV) solar

ANNUAL PRODUCTION: 22 MWh per unit (less the energy used by the drone battery)

OTHER SOCIAL CO-BENEFITS: water harvesting for irrigation

Unfold **is an energy and water** harvesting artwork that irrigates the landscape of Spinelli Park while generating renewable energy and agriculture for urban life. The project is inspired by Mannheim's reputation as the "city of inventions" — the bicycle, automobile, and tractor are well known examples — and by its most recognizable symbol, the 60-meter tall Wasserturm (water tower) designed by Gustav Halmhuber, the winner of a nationwide design competition in 1885.

Mannheim is one of the sunniest places in Germany with an annual solar radiation potential of 1,200 kWh/m^2, which is about two thirds that of southern Spain and one and a half times that of Scandinavia. Mannheim also experiences high humidity, which can be harvested and collected as water for irrigation, recreation, and even for drinking. Taking advantage of these two local conditions, *Unfold* incorporates an organic photovoltaic skin and a solar-driven hygroscopic water harvesting system.

The water harvesting device is made of semi-transparent material surrounded by the OPV skin. The device harvests water from the air through an ancient method. During the night, a sorbent material in the device captures water molecules by physical adsorption from the air. The water molecules in the sorbent are desorbed under the heating of sunlight during the day. Through this process, the water vapor is recondensed, liquefied, and collected within the unit.

Inspired by Dyson® products, each *Unfold* unit incorporates a bladeless air propulsion system that is composed mainly of impellers, loops, a battery, and a surrounding water tank, which are all hidden from view by stainless steel cladding. After a day of exposure to the sunlight, the collection tank slowly fills up with harvested water vapor from the night before. As it fills, the OPV skin folds into a compact formation that triggers the release of the artwork from its charging mast in the early evening. In its drone manifestation, each *Unfold* unit follows a programmed path across the site providing artificial rain to irrigate gardens, trees, and planting beds. The unit returns to its charging mast and unfolds into its full shape once all of the collected water has been distributed. The sorbent materials are re-cooled during the night for the next water vapor capture cycle. Each unit can harvest more than 250,000 liters of water per year.

When installed in a private garden, one *Unfold* unit can save water and electricity for a family — providing an experience of joy and wonder at sunset as the artificial rain cloud roams overhead.

At night *Unfold* drones return to their home masts after an evening of irrigating the landscape. Once attached, they slowly expand into their longest form, signifying that they are ready to begin receiving the sun's rays the next morning to generate clean energy for the city. The daily ritual provides a dynamic and entertaining experience for those who live near Spinelli Park.

Unfold (continued)

Energy harvesting process

When the sun rises in the morning, the organic photovoltaic skin is at its greatest length, ready to capture solar energy. Certain wavelengths of sunlight penetrate the skin to reach the water harvesting system.

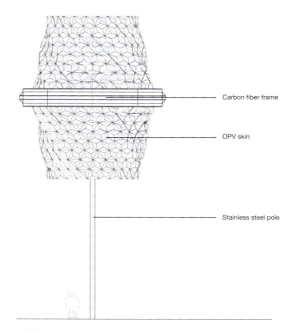

Carbon fiber frame

OPV skin

Stainless steel pole

Elevation

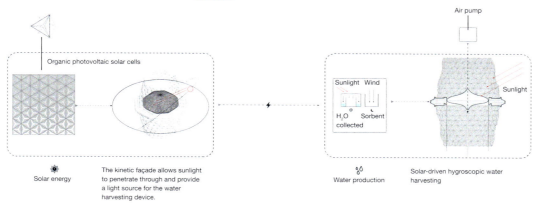

Organic photovoltaic solar cells

Air pump

Sunlight

Solar energy

The kinetic façade allows sunlight to penetrate through and provide a light source for the water harvesting device.

Water production

Solar-driven hygroscopic water harvesting

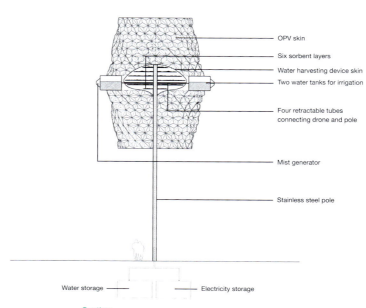

OPV skin
Six sorbent layers
Water harvesting device skin
Two water tanks for irrigation

Four retractable tubes connecting drone and pole

Mist generator

Stainless steel pole

Water storage — Electricity storage

Section

102

Inspired by folding paper, the installation is designed to be retractable. The folding and unfolding follows the process of the solar-driven hygroscopic water harvesting. When the water to its most compact shape. This sends a signal to the drone that it is ready to take off and irrigate the landscape. When irrigation is finished, the drone returns back to its origin to charge. The OPV skin

GIRASOLI

DESIGNER: Antonio Maccà

ENERGY TECHNOLOGY: laminated monocrystalline photovoltaic solar (similar to Solaxess™)

ANNUAL PRODUCTION: 170 MWh (0.5 MWh at residential scale)

OTHER SOCIAL CO-BENEFITS: shaded public space

GIRASOLI is a photovoltaic sculpture representing a sunflower, one of nature's most simple and fascinating symbols of beauty and resilience.

Like the flower from which it draws inspiration, *GIRASOLI* rotates and tilts, tracking the light of the sun and transforming its flow into renewable energy. Sensitive to the environment, the heliotropic sculpture performs both the rotation of Earth around its own axis and its revolution around the Sun. The round solar face incorporates monocrystalline silicon photovoltaic cells with a custom lamination of high-transmittance white nano-film that is applied over the module during assembly, concealing any hint of the solar technology behind. The lamination only slightly reduces conversion efficiency, which is more than overcome by the tracking mechanism.

The project proposes the same model scaled to different dimensions, ranging from a sculptural pavilion in a civic park to a design object in a residential garden. At its civic scale, *GIRASOLI* is a venue for cultural events for both residents and visitors throughout the year. The main structure is a phototropic pavilion with an inclined cover above a slowly shifting venue. It moves on a circular rail track, the circumference of which delineates an area for recreation, performance, educational activities, or gardening. The round rail track symbolizes the outermost circumference of the sun's path. The cardinal points and the position of the sun at sunrise and sunset on the 21st of each month of the year are marked along the path, highlighting solstices and equinoxes.

The pavilion creates a large mobile arch representing a rotating portal to the park. The whole structure requires only two support points — one is fixed in the center and the other follows the sun, leaving a large unobstructed and shaded space below for social activities.

At its residential scale, a smaller *GIRASOLI* supports activities like urban farming and private gardening, rotating to provide clean energy in much the same way.

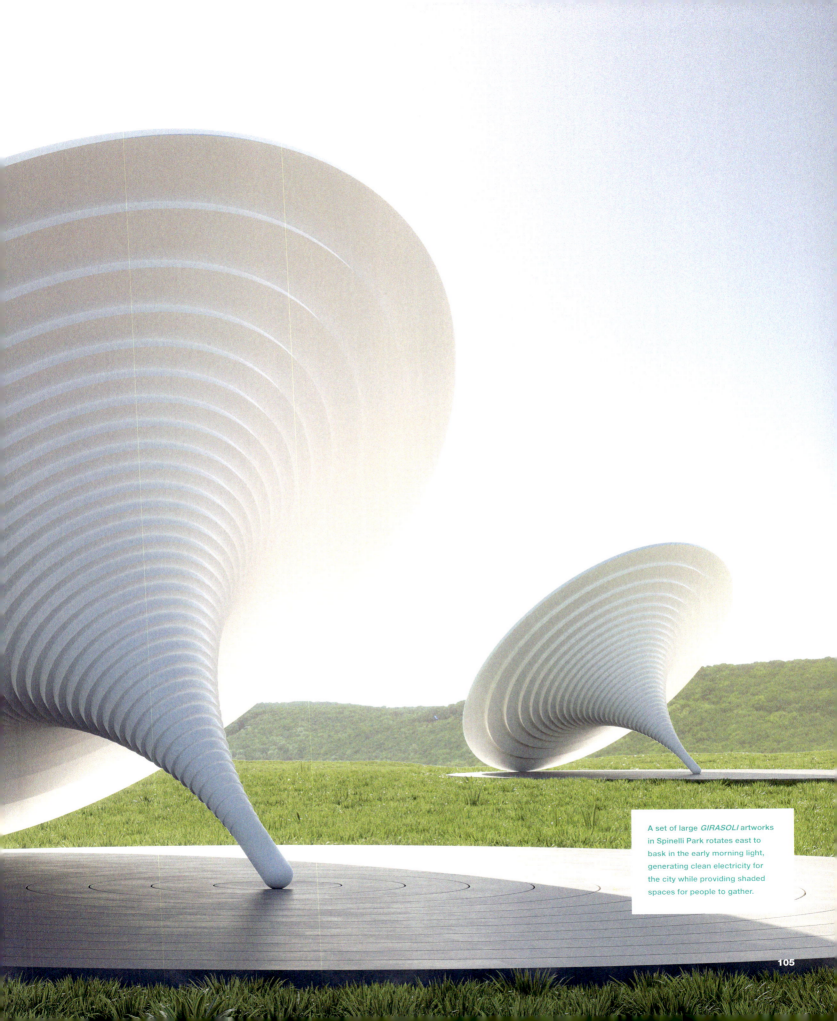

A set of large *GIRASOLI* artworks in Spinelli Park rotates east to bask in the early morning light, generating clean electricity for the city while providing shaded spaces for people to gather.

GIRASOLI (continued)

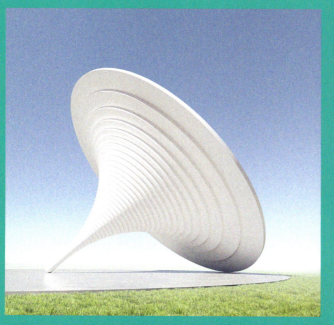

At its civic scale, *GIRASOLI* is a phototropic pavilion with an inclined cover above a flexible venue. *GIRASOLI* has a rotational and telescopic support structure that allows it to orient the circular flat surface, composed of photovoltaic panels, toward the sunlight.

At its residential scale, *GIRASOLI* is a tilting and spinning solar panel providing clean energy for activities such as urban farming and gardening.

Trees and Seesaws

DESIGNER: Yongsu Choung

ENERGY TECHNOLOGY: monocrystalline solar photovoltaic modules with color lamination (similar to Kromatix™ by SwissINSO), kinetic energy harvesting

ANNUAL PRODUCTION: 200 MWh

OTHER SOCIAL CO-BENEFITS: playground, exercise space for public health, public space for gathering and events

Trees and Seesaws is an eco-friendly open structure that provides spaces for public activities and recreation in Spinelli Park. The energy-generating artwork co-exists with a glade of trees relocated from BUGA 23 (the German Federal Horticulture Show).

Colorful louvers above comprise 1,450 square meters of color-laminated solar modules that provide a comfortable microclimate in the park. Twenty-three tree-like vertical columns support the long-span beams and compression rings that allow the natural trees to grow up above the canopy uninterrupted.

Visitors enjoy playing on the seesaws that are installed at the base of each column, perhaps blissfully unaware that their play is generating additional clean energy. Interpretive displays engage the more curious park-goer, illustrating the kinetic energy-harvesting dynamos and the battery energy storage that is integrated into the workings of each seesaw.

Trees and Seesaws is a place for visitors to enjoy the landscape of Spinelli Park, to generate clean energy, and to improve public health and happiness, while supporting the larger goals of the Climate Corridor to bring fresh air into the city.

Smaller versions of the artwork can be made with one structural column for installation in residential gardens or pocket parks. The artwork reminds us that the ultimate goal of technical solutions for renewable energy generation is to achieve symbiosis with nature.

Partial section

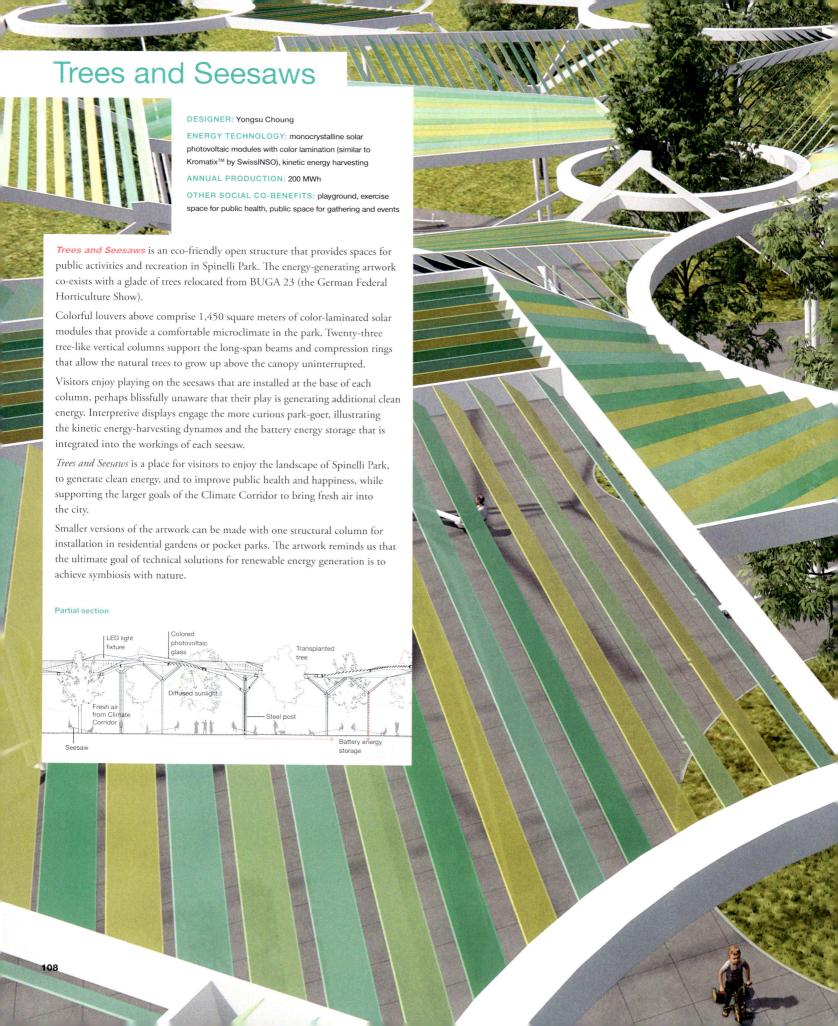

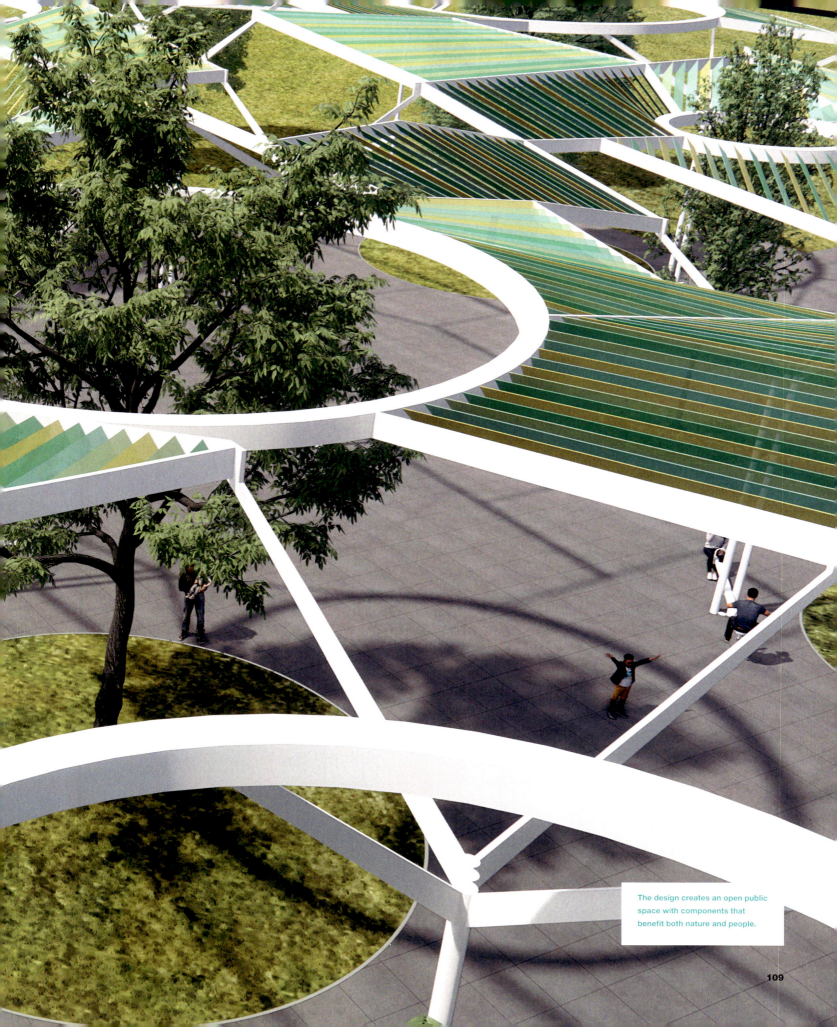

The design creates an open public space with components that benefit both nature and people.

Trees and Seesaws (continued)

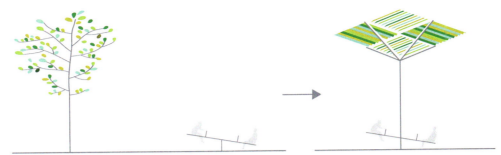

Inspiration from nature and play

Harvesting energy from a tree-like structure and seesaw

Transplant existing trees at the site to create civic public space.

Twenty-three tree-like structures and seesaws used by visitors.

Linear and circular beams connect vertical structures.

Green tinted PV panels generate energy in harmony with trees.

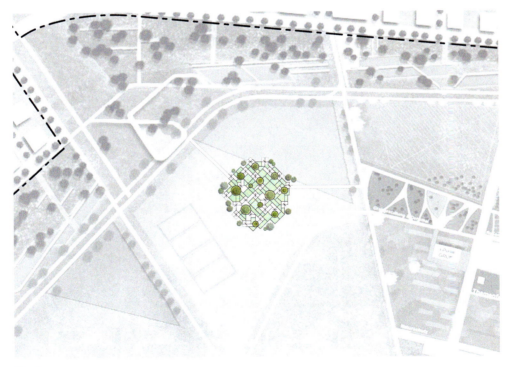

Site plan

View from south

Construction detail

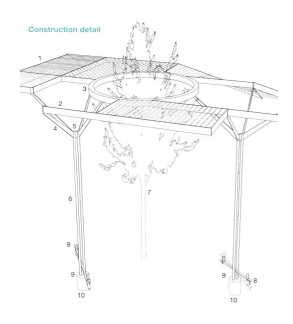

1. Colored photovoltaic glass (shades of green)
2. Aluminum frame (50 mm x 300 mm)
3. Circular aluminum frame (300 mm x 300 mm)
4. Diagonal beam support
5. LED light fixture
6. Steel pipe
7. Transplanted tree
8. Kinetic energy harvesting seesaw
9. Base plate
10. Precast concrete pile foundation

The kinetic energy generated by visitors using the seesaws is converted into electricity and stored in a battery buried underground.

Artee

DESIGNERS: Jonathan Hernandez Lopez, Lorenz Riedel, Nawapan Suntorachai, Maria Matheou, Felipe Romero

ENERGY TECHNOLOGY: tinted translucent thin-film solar photovoltaic with pneumatic tracking, kinetic energy paving bubbles

ANNUAL PRODUCTION: 100 MWh (art pavilion), 1,700 MWh (solar thin-film towers), 5 MWh (kinetic energy harvesting pavers)

OTHER SOCIAL CO-BENEFITS: sheltered public gathering space, interactive play

Artee **demonstrates a high-performance** adaptive kinetic solar pavilion with sun-tracking solar thin-film towers and energy-harvesting landscapes. It actively engages the community to participate in a regenerative urban environment.

An adaptive art pavilion at the main crossing of the pedestrian and bicycle pathways provides open-air shelter for people to meet and interact. The pavilion, covered with organic solar thin-film, uses a pneumatic system to transform its shape, maximizing solar energy production throughout the day and year. The building structure of the adaptive pavilion consists of inflatable tensairity beams defined as ribs connected with an inner and outer ring. This ultra-light and flexible structure allows the pavilion to change shape by adjusting the air pressure inside the individual tensairity ribs.

The organic shape and material construction of the pavilion is an homage to the technologically advanced Multihalle by architects Frei Otto and Carlfried Mutschler, which was built for BUGA 1975, the last time that the German Bundesgartenschau was hosted in Mannheim. The Multihalle is being revitalized and will be on display at BUGA 23 within the part of the event being held in Luisenpark.

In addition to the central art pavilion, sun-tracking solar thin-film towers are scattered throughout the park. Using the same tensairity structural elements as the pavilion, the petals of each tower track the sun to maximize solar energy gain, while at the same time maximizing shade for park visitors. When the solar irradiance decreases from heavy clouds or after sunset, the petals fold in to become sculptural shapes as air is drawn down from the structural armatures.

Between the solar towers are ETFE bubble pavers that harvest electricity from the activity of park visitors who are enticed to meander through the complex curving forms.

Offsite in German kleingärten, the solar thin-film towers function as single elements. They represent an aesthetic type of green energy production in an ultra-light and material-friendly system that can work at residential scale as well as on a civic scale, like Spinelli Park, when aggregated in large numbers.

Artee (continued)

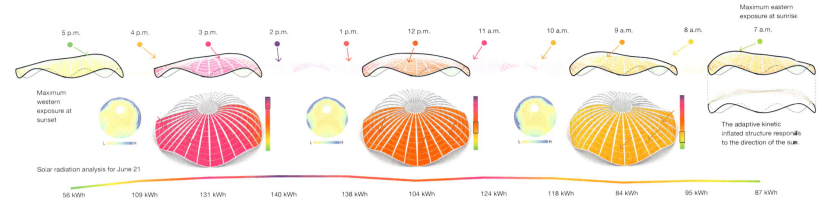

Solar radiation analysis for June 21

The tensairity structure allows the entire form to shift throughout the day, exposing the greatest surface area to direct sunlight.

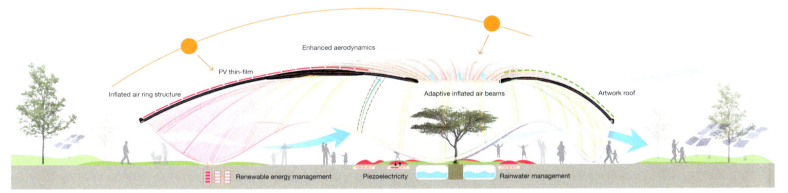

Section through the pavilion

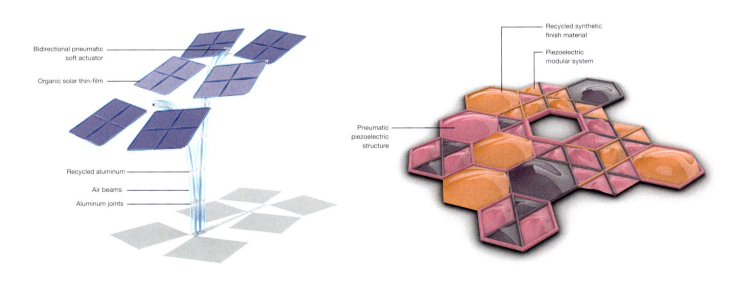

Adaptive kinetic tower in the open position during the day

Piezoelectric paver structure

Kleingarten scale

Adaptive kinetic tower in the closed position at night

BAU(M): The Fractal Tree

DESIGNER: Mikołaj Ćwikła
ENERGY TECHNOLOGY: bismuth nanocrystal solar cells
ANNUAL PRODUCTION: 0.5 MWh per tree
(180 MWh from 360 trees)
OTHER SOCIAL CO-BENEFITS: water harvesting

A balance between function and form should be considered while designing an urban energy landscape. The shape of the landscape should be utilitarian enough to provide a useful service and yet its form should be a timeless gesture. In an effort to achieve this balance, the tree is the perfect source of inspiration — a recognizable symbol that provides a host of ecosystem services and has evolved to efficiently harness the energy of the sun.

BAU(M): The Fractal Tree is made from sustainable materials, including natural bamboo and recycled metal assembled in the form of a fractal truss to minimize material use and maximize structural integrity. Rather than competing with nature, the design learns from, supports, and blends with nature, while enhancing the range of ecosystem services that nature can provide.

The composition of the BAU(M) trees in Spinelli Park follows a pattern of three density typologies, reflecting patterns observed in nature: dense, semi-dense, and free-standing.

Each BAU(M) leaf contains the bismuth nanocrystal cells developed by CORDIS EU, which are thin, lightweight, and less expensive than conventional solar cells. They are mounted on movable hinged joints to tree rods, allowing them to flutter in the wind. As the flow of clean air from the Climate Corridor is channeled into the city between these various clusters of BAU(M) trees, the leaves cast dynamic shadows in the park, reducing the heat island effect while captivating the imaginations of park-goers. Polyester mesh located in the trunk of each BAU(M) gathers water and channels it to the surrounding rain gardens.

Medium and large *BAU(M)* trees interspersed with smaller scale bush-like varieties generate electricity and harvest water for Spinelli Park. Their shimmering photovoltaic leaves are a consistent presence throughout the seasons.

BAU(M): The Fractal Tree (continued)

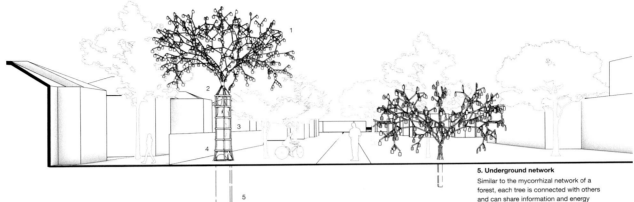

5. Underground network
Similar to the mycorrhizal network of a forest, each tree is connected with others and can share information and energy between them.

1. Solar cells
Ultra-thin bismuth nanocrystal photovoltaic cells are attached with hinged joints to the rigid bamboo structure, allowing them to move in the wind like natural leaves.

2. Primary joint and vertical structure
The primary joint is made from strong and rigid recycled plastic. Its purpose is to connect the trunk with the canopy.

3. Trunk
Rigid connectors made from 3D printed recycled plastic attach to bamboo lintels and posts.

4. Water catchment system
Polyester mesh spanning between posts and secured with organic rope collects water from condensing atmospheric vapor.

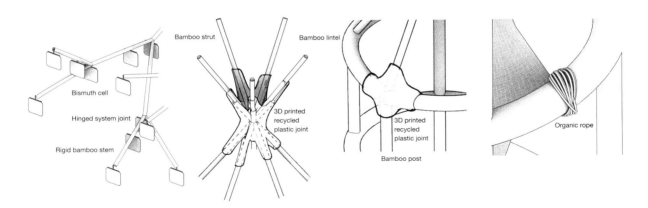

1. Inner city scale
Reaching into the surrounding city, every green lane, small park, and private garden can accommodate a BAU(M) installation and derive energy artfully from the sun.

2. Forest and the city
BAU(M) artworks merge with natural habitats, providing additional moisture during dry seasons and creating cool microclimates in the city park. All of the components are interchangeable allowing the artworks to be made larger or smaller to adapt to their surroundings.

3. Crossroads
At the very center of the park visitors discover a connection between the past and future of Spinelli Park.

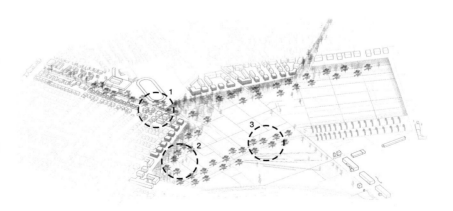

With interchangeable parts, the installations can expand over time. In this way, *BAU(M)* and plants grow symbiotically.

Bloom: Energy Infrastructure as an Ecosystem Catalyst in a Dry Land

DESIGNERS: Muhammad Iqbal Tawakal, Melvina Pramadya Puspahati
ENERGY TECHNOLOGY: solar photovoltaic
ANNUAL PRODUCTION: 3 MWh per unit (100 MWh over the entire site)
OTHER SOCIAL CO-BENEFITS: 10 liters per day of water from atmospheric water generation, public gardens

As a consequence of climate change, the summer is getting hotter and dryer in Mannheim and the surrounding Rhine-Neckar region. *Bloom* is a hydro-photovoltaic panel that combines solar cells with hygroscopic materials that pull water vapor from heated air. The hybrid system is an ecosystem catalyst in a city designed to generate electrical power while keeping the surrounding landscape thriving and flourishing during dry seasons.

The land artwork provides shade and protection for park-goers, plants, and wildlife. The microclimate generated by *Blooms*' water generation creates a cool place of refuge for city dwellers in the summer months and a comfortable environment for learning activities on site. *Bloom* is designed to meet a circular use of materials taking advantage of reused demolition waste from the former Spinelli Barracks.

Each *Bloom* module is an extruded hexagonal shape — a waffle structure with sustainable plywood cladding — inspired by the structure of a beehive. At the center of each unit is a twelve square meter solar panel paired with a solar-powered hydropanel-type atmospheric water generator. The hydropanel uses the sun to make water by drawing humid air through a solar vaporization chamber and onto a hygroscopic material that absorbs water particles in the air and generates water droplets. The water then enters a moist chamber where organic materials filter the water slowly into the surrounding landscape.

In the summer, the main unit becomes a canopy and moisture chamber for water production. In the winter, the plywood cladding is replaced with translucent curtains hung from the eaves, turning the entire area into a greenhouse. A small, mobile unit adopts the principle of a hybrid solar and water system for use in private gardens.

Bloom: Energy Infrastructure as an Ecosystem Catalyst in a Dry Land
(continued)

Summer mode, as a canopy for sun shade. Winter mode, as a mobile greenhouse.

Primary canopy

Smaller mobile units in three sizes are scattered between the primary canopies and placed according to the height of surrounding vegetation. Each smaller mobile unit contains all of the components of the primary canopy.

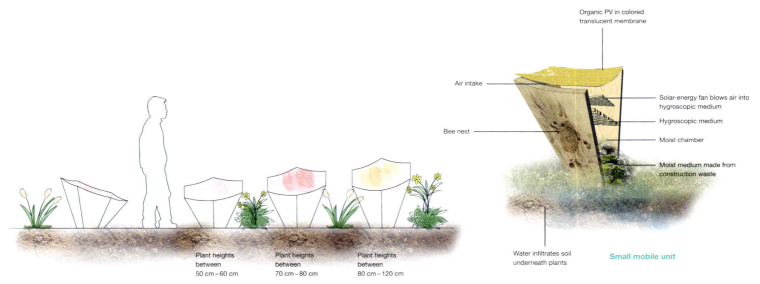

Small mobile unit

Section diagram

Energiebaum

DESIGNERS: Minu Joshi, Unmesh Lele, Ajay Vaidya

ENERGY TECHNOLOGY: thermophotovoltaic (TPV), vertical axis wind turbine (VAWT)

ANNUAL PRODUCTION: 2.5 MWh per unit

OTHER SOCIAL CO-BENEFITS: 18,000 liters of water per unit per year, electrical device charging, assists food production by heating local greenhouses

Learning from nature's graceful and functional forms, *Energiebaum* redefines the idea of the tree — harvesting the energy of the sun, collecting water in its leaves, and creating beautiful dynamic spaces by way of its relationship to its surroundings. The artwork blends into Spinelli Park, complementing the natural trees within clusters or as individual units, and delighting visitors with its ever-changing form.

Energiebaum incorporates thermophotovoltaic (TPV) technology into each of the narrow blades that comprise its two large leaf-like forms. As the sun hits the TPV leaf blades, its energy is converted into electricity. Rainwater collected by the leaves is passed behind each photovoltaic cell, drawing away heat and increasing the efficiency of energy conversion. The captured heat helps to regulate the temperature of nearby greenhouses.

The large leaf-shape forms are also designed to catch the wind in the manner of a vertical axis wind turbine. As gentle breezes flow through the Climate Corridor, it causes the tree canopy to spin atop its trunk, sending additional electricity to the city grid. As the wind picks up speed, centrifugal force widens the leaf canopy and creates dynamic shadows on the landscape. Grouping the *Energiebaum* installations into clusters helps to increase the energy output as wake wind effects improve the performance of adjacent downstream units.

At night, a soft glowing pink light is reflected downward by the 450 *Energiebaum* artworks around Spinelli Park, providing safe illumination and keeping the skies dark. The rings that mark the dripline of the canopy at the ground level pulse slowly to a rhythm determined by the amount of energy generated during the day. This makes for an even more dynamic setting while connecting park-goers to the energy they consume.

Energiebaum (continued)

Energiebaum functions as thermophotovoltaic (TPV) collectors during the day.

Energiebaum functions as wind turbines during low light.

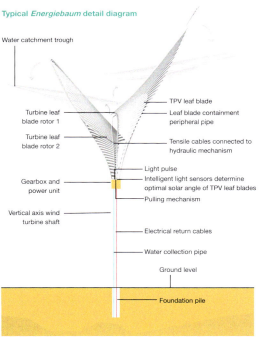

Typical *Energiebaum* detail diagram

- Water catchment trough
- Turbine leaf blade rotor 1
- Turbine leaf blade rotor 2
- Gearbox and power unit
- Vertical axis wind turbine shaft
- TPV leaf blade
- Leaf blade containment peripheral pipe
- Tensile cables connected to hydraulic mechanism
- Light pulse
- Intelligent light sensors determine optimal solar angle of TPV leaf blades
- Pulling mechanism
- Electrical return cables
- Water collection pipe
- Ground level
- Foundation pile

Art boosts local economies in five key ways: attracting visitors, creating jobs and developing skills, attracting and retaining businesses, revitalizing places, and developing talent. *Energiebaum* adds to this list by generating clean energy and water for the City of Mannheim.

The *Energiebaum* shaft
The shaft carries the water line to recharge the water directed from the leaf blades. It also houses the electrical return cables to direct the electricity generated to the required destination.

Intelligent light sensors
The light sensors determine the optimal solar angle for the TPV leaf blades ensuring maximum solar radiation on the required surfaces throughout the year.

The water catchment trough
The TPV leaf blade doubles as a water catchment trough which directs the rainwater and melted snow back to the ground thereby increasing the groundwater table.

The vertical axis wind turbine rotors
Depending on the time of day and the amount of solar radiation, the TPV blades change their position and become a vertical axis wind turbine enabling continuous energy generation.

Solar catchment
The TPV leaf blade directs the solar radiation to solar collectors below it, thus generating heat energy and converting it to electricity via photons.

Energy Generation

DESIGNERS: Kazia Rodrigo, Peter North, Alissa North, Fernanda de Carvalho Nunes

ENERGY TECHNOLOGY: high altitude wind power (HAWP), organic photovoltaic (OPV) solar, pumped micro-hydro energy storage, kinetic energy pavers

ANNUAL PRODUCTION: 8,000 MWh

OTHER SOCIAL CO-BENEFITS: play and exercise spaces, charging for personal devices, reforested landscape

Energy Generation democratizes accessibility to renewable energy resources by using the energy of young people within an urban playscape to help power the city. Four technologies and a program of reforestation come together to create an interactive, inspirational, playful, purposeful, and productive landscape.

The park features solar, hydro, wind, and kinetic energy sculptures. It provides an educational, inspirational, and interactive experience where renewable energy is embedded in public space as elements of wayfinding, sculpture, shade, and playground.

By experiencing the wonder of *Energy Generation*, visitors will be inspired to bring smaller-scale renewable energy technologies to their own gardens and advocate for their implementation around the city. Various smaller-scale versions of the playful infrastructures are presented as models for residential use.

High altitude wind power (HAWP) turbines — able to gather more wind than average wind turbines due to the consistency of wind at higher elevations — are anchored on the southwestern corner of Spinelli Park and act as wayfinding elements guiding visitors into the park. Some of the energy generated from these powerful turbines is directed to pumped micro-hydro storage tanks at the top of the project's water features. When additional power is desired, the water is released to run vortex hydro turbines that are efficient even under low pressure. The release of water has the added benefit in summer months of cooling the surrounding air.

Stretched fabric umbrellas and a pavilion space are made from thin and flexible organic photovoltaic (OPV) solar material to provide shade and protection from the elements along with clean electricity. The paths, playscapes, skate park, and BMX park incorporate kinetic energy pavers with visual displays of power generation that encourage park-goers of all ages to run and jump as they convert their human energy into useful power.

The artwork incorporates seven diverse types of native trees that increase carbon sequestration, cool the city, improve air quality, and reduce stormwater runoff.

Der Bienenstock (The Hive)

DESIGNERS: Héctor Fernando Paredes Gutiérrez, Luis Ariel Zúñiga Guerrero, Alejandro Israel Muñiz

ENERGY TECHNOLOGY: concentrator photovoltaic (CPV) solar, geothermal, kinetic energy harvesting

ANNUAL PRODUCTION: 150 MWh

OTHER SOCIAL CO-BENEFITS: rainwater harvesting, food production, insect and pollinator habitat, shaded public gathering space

"Over there, where butterflies and bees play, I walk." — Hölderlin

Der Bienenstock attempts to evoke the same sense of landscape that the German poet Hölderlin suggests in this simple turn of phrase. It is a beautiful place where people can interact harmoniously with local nature, small animals, and plants inside a symbiotic hive. The structure generates and manages energy in a flexible way to suit different site conditions and support the traditional practice of the community garden.

The artwork is inspired by the natural geometric form of the honeycomb, optimal in its use of material and adaptable to a variety of conditions and contexts. Each module consists of a photovoltaic dish, a funnel that collects rainwater, a translucent membrane that works as a greenhouse, and a shelter for insects and small animals. Kinetic wind energy harvesting modules enhance the windflow direction of the Climate Corridor while generating additional clean electricity.

The organic structure is fabricated from natural materials and supports an expansion of urban agriculture. While specifically designed to integrate into Spinelli Park, the modular design can be implemented in other contexts. *Der Bienenstock* provides a vast public space for many activities, such as walking, running, outdoor training, and even public events like concerts, urban galleries, and shows. Its form serves to direct windflows and combat the urban heat island effect.

Solar production is accomplished by means of concentrator photovoltaics with dual-axis sun tracking. Each solar module includes many hollows integrated into the structure ready to be used by birds, bees, squirrels, and other small urban fauna. Filaments made of composite carbon fiber power a piezoelectric system that gently harvests additional electricity from the wind. Ground source heat energy is harvested by means of a geothermal loop to warm the greenhouse spaces and improve food production.

Der Bienenstock (The Hive) (continued)

Der Bienenstock is a symbiotic structure that brings together plants, animals, humans, and the environment.

Der Bienenstock creates a hive structure that generates and manages energy in a flexible way, in order to suit different site conditions.

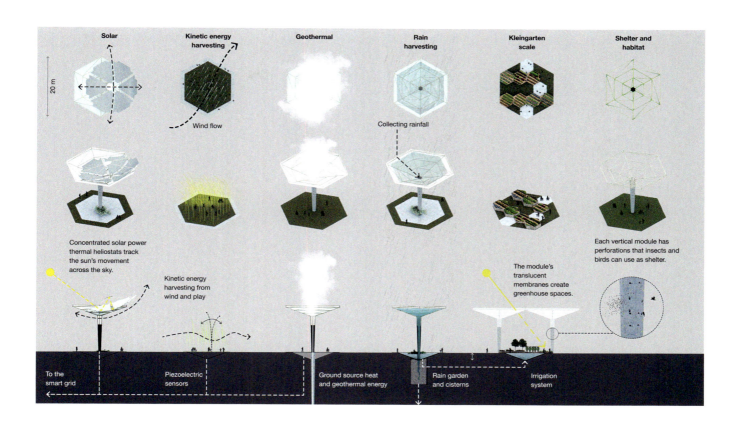

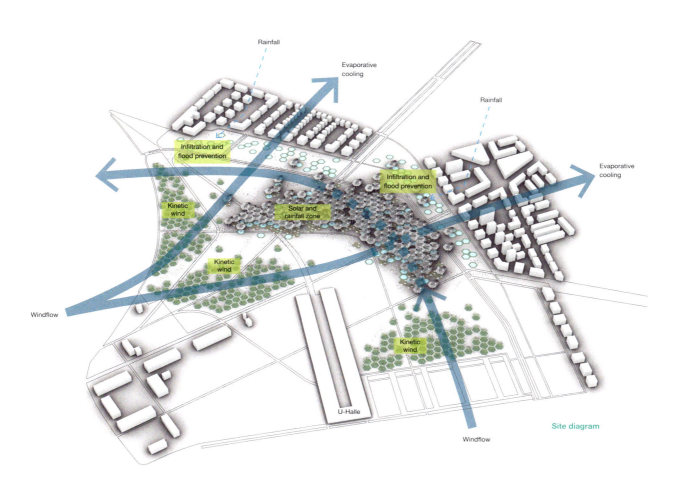

Site diagram

Sky Wings

DESIGNER: Islambek Yeshbekov

ENERGY TECHNOLOGY: solar photovoltaic, triboelectric nanogenerators (TENG), kinetic energy harvesting from wind and human activities, micro-hydro from rainwater, microbial fuel cells (MFC)

ANNUAL PRODUCTION: 1,410 MWh

OTHER SOCIAL CO-BENEFITS: stormwater harvesting for irrigation, food and beverage concessions, exercise equipment for public health, spaces for meeting and performance

From a distance, *Sky Wings* seems to dissolve into the landscape, its low-profile forms casting shimmering reflections of the grass and clouds. As visitors get closer, they see the geometry of the artwork as a series of four rhomboid kites that resemble a flock of birds taking flight. When they reach *Sky Wings*, they discover a place of creativity, thoughtful reflection, and recreation for people of all ages.

In the foreground plaza, planted triangular areas tilt up to reveal concession pavilions that provide refreshments to park-goers. Within the soil of the pavilion's living roof, microbial fuel cells continuously generate electricity to power building operations during the day and site lighting throughout the night.

The roof of the main pavilions comprises a large array of solar modules that also incorporate a cutting edge technology that generates electricity from rainwater. Using a thin graphene layer the modules harness the charge difference between the sodium and potassium salts within the water and the subtle force of each raindrop using triboelectric nanogenerators (TENG). After the rain has given its energy to the hybrid solar modules, it makes its way through micro-hydro turbines and is collected in cisterns for irrigation use.

On the ceiling of the pavilions, thousands of small, mirrored aluminum plates flutter like the surface of water, animated by the wind that flows from the surrounding forested hills and into the city through Spinelli Park. As the plates move in glistening patterns of reflection, they create a delightful visual effect and generate additional electricity with piezoelectric actuators located within each mounting hinge.

Protected by the shade of the pavilions, exercise equipment such as stationary bicycles and ellipticals generates additional electricity for public charging stations. *Sky Wings* is a unique place for people to explore and benefit from renewable energy in all of its many wonderful facets!

Sky Wings (continued)

Sky Wings is designed as a gathering space for people of all ages.

Piezoelectric plates generate electricity from the wind that flows through the park while creating shimmering dynamic visual effects.

Sky Wings is designed in the shape of a rhomboid kite and resembles a flock of flying birds.

Speak Up

DESIGNERS: Azhar Mussinova, Akmaral Kussainova

ENERGY TECHNOLOGY: solar photovoltaic, piezoelectric micro wind turbines, kinetic energy pavers, triboelectric rain energy harvesters

ANNUAL PRODUCTION: 500 MWh

OTHER SOCIAL CO-BENEFITS: educational and performance venue, shaded gathering space, rainwater harvesting, electronic device charging

At the crossroads in the northwest section of Spinelli Park, almost hidden behind glades of trees, lies a magical experience of energy and art in the city — a peaceful area, a common picnic space, a place to relax, and a place to meet.

The moon jellyfish, one of the most energy-efficient organisms on the planet, serves as the inspiration for the perimeter gathering spaces, while an amalgamation of starfish and seashells form the amphitheater, the heart of the oasis-like installation.

A range of cultural and educational events take place in the central amphitheater of *Speak Up*, providing a space for visitors to speak their mind. Programming, such as conferences, master classes, exhibitions, stand-ups, debates, community gatherings, performances, and more, offer a place to overcome the fear of sharing one's voice.

Both the central amphitheater and the perimeter gathering spaces are fabricated with regenerative technologies embedded into the form. These include triboelectric rainwater harvesting collectors, wind harvesting microturbines, photovoltaic solar cells, and piezoelectric sound sensors. Piezoelectric energy-harvesting pavers supply lighting and power audio installations. Three polygonal-shaped speakers installed around the periphery broadcast the events taking place in the amphitheater for those who are enjoying the outdoor space.

The amphitheater also serves as a recreational area where city dwellers can work quietly or take lessons. Throughout the artwork visitors will find sockets for connecting various gadgets to the power grid, tables for laptops and books, soft pillows, and free Wi-Fi. Beautiful illumination integrated into walking paths smoothly guides people around the park after dark.

Speak Up (continued)

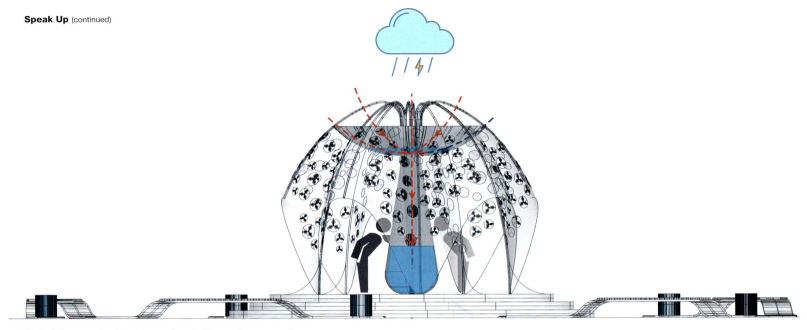

The buildings contain rainwater harvesting collectors, wind harvesting microturbines, photovoltaic solar panels, piezoelectric sound sensors, and piezoelectric pavers to generate energy to supply lighting and stereo installations.

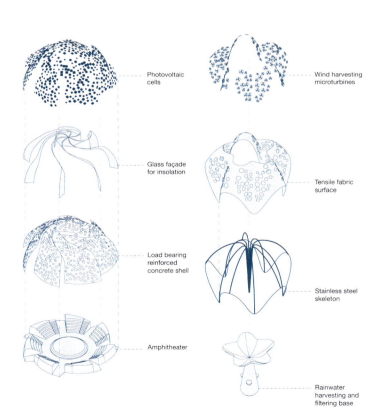

- Photovoltaic cells
- Glass façade for insolation
- Load bearing reinforced concrete shell
- Amphitheater
- Wind harvesting microturbines
- Tensile fabric surface
- Stainless steel skeleton
- Rainwater harvesting and filtering base

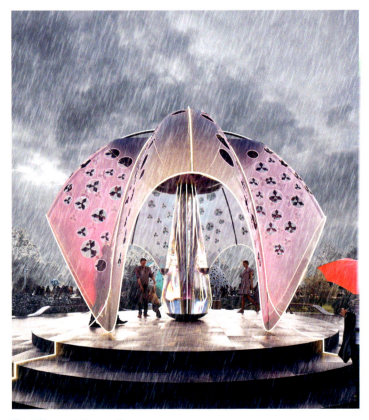

Speak Up repeats the smooth forms of the moon jellyfish, possibly one of the most energy-efficient living organisms on the planet.

While jellyfish art installations serve as the soul of the project, the amphitheater in the center is undoubtedly its heart.

Created as a symbiosis of a starfish and a seashell, it is the semantic and compositional center of this little oasis.

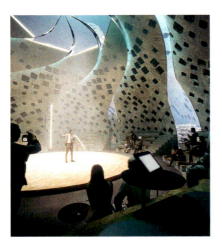

The amphitheater is designed to host cultural and educational events that provide a platform for visitors to use their voices.

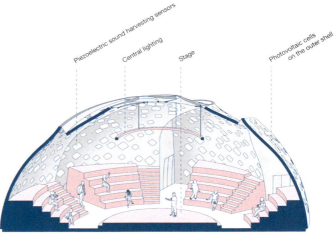

Amphitheater section

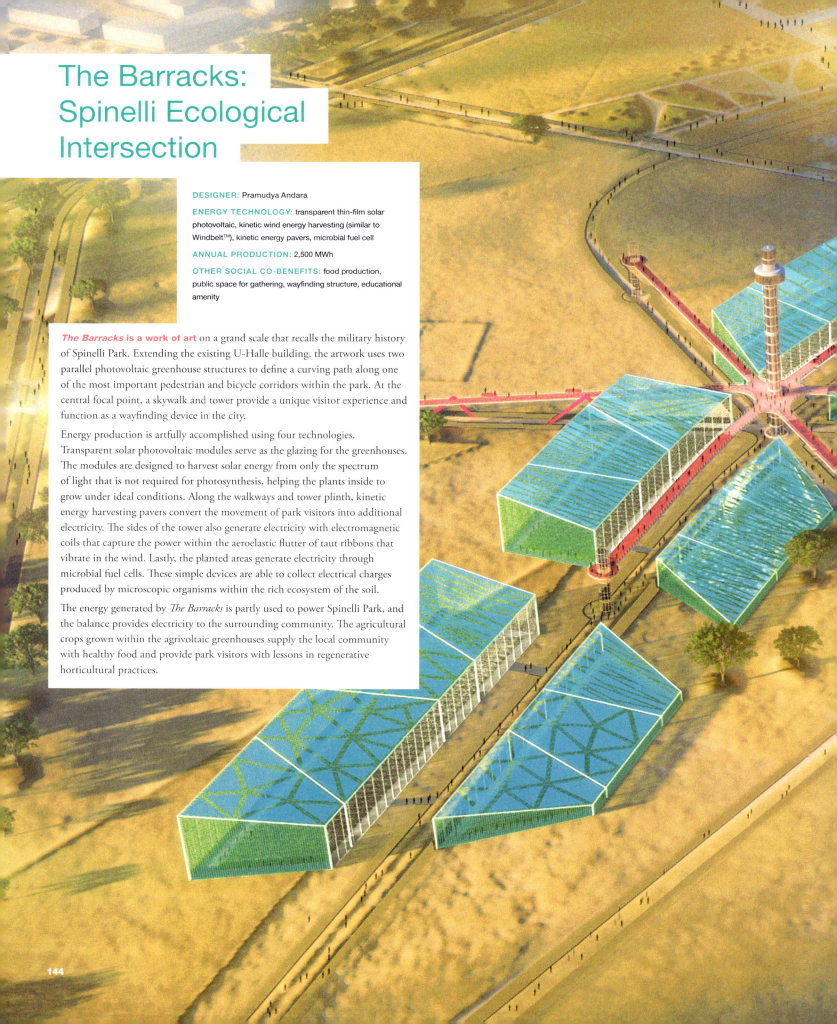

The Barracks: Spinelli Ecological Intersection

DESIGNER: Pramudya Andara

ENERGY TECHNOLOGY: transparent thin-film solar photovoltaic, kinetic wind energy harvesting (similar to Windbelt™), kinetic energy pavers, microbial fuel cell

ANNUAL PRODUCTION: 2,500 MWh

OTHER SOCIAL CO-BENEFITS: food production, public space for gathering, wayfinding structure, educational amenity

The Barracks is a work of art on a grand scale that recalls the military history of Spinelli Park. Extending the existing U-Halle building, the artwork uses two parallel photovoltaic greenhouse structures to define a curving path along one of the most important pedestrian and bicycle corridors within the park. At the central focal point, a skywalk and tower provide a unique visitor experience and function as a wayfinding device in the city.

Energy production is artfully accomplished using four technologies. Transparent solar photovoltaic modules serve as the glazing for the greenhouses. The modules are designed to harvest solar energy from only the spectrum of light that is not required for photosynthesis, helping the plants inside to grow under ideal conditions. Along the walkways and tower plinth, kinetic energy harvesting pavers convert the movement of park visitors into additional electricity. The sides of the tower also generate electricity with electromagnetic coils that capture the power within the aeroelastic flutter of taut ribbons that vibrate in the wind. Lastly, the planted areas generate electricity through microbial fuel cells. These simple devices are able to collect electrical charges produced by microscopic organisms within the rich ecosystem of the soil.

The energy generated by *The Barracks* is partly used to power Spinelli Park, and the balance provides electricity to the surrounding community. The agricultural crops grown within the agrivoltaic greenhouses supply the local community with healthy food and provide park visitors with lessons in regenerative horticultural practices.

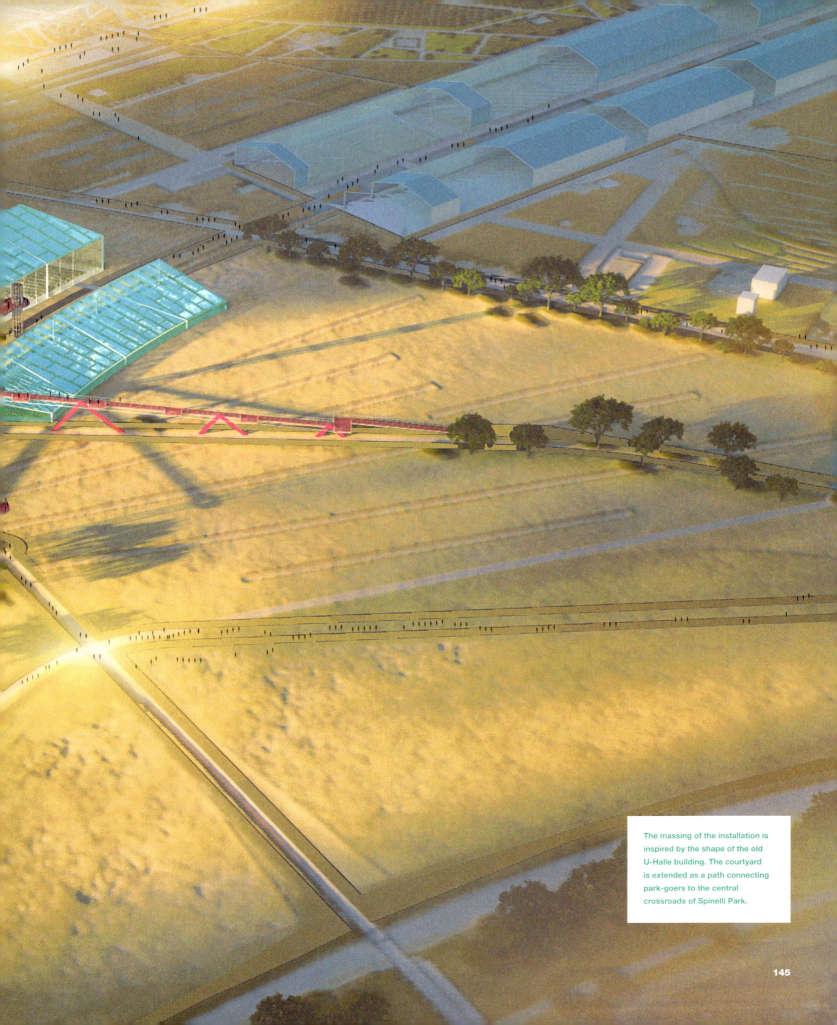

The massing of the installation is inspired by the shape of the old U-Halle building. The courtyard is extended as a path connecting park-goers to the central crossroads of Spinelli Park.

The Barracks: Spinelli Ecological Intersection (continued)

Rows of lettuce grow beneath the red glow of the photovoltaic greenhouse glass.

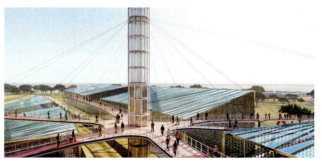

The energy generated by *The Barracks* is used to power Spinelli Park, public facilities, and nearby buildings and housing, while the agricultural crops supply the local community with food.

Visitors to Spinelli Park wander through rows of solar photovoltaic greenhouses on their way to experience the 50-meter tall observation tower.

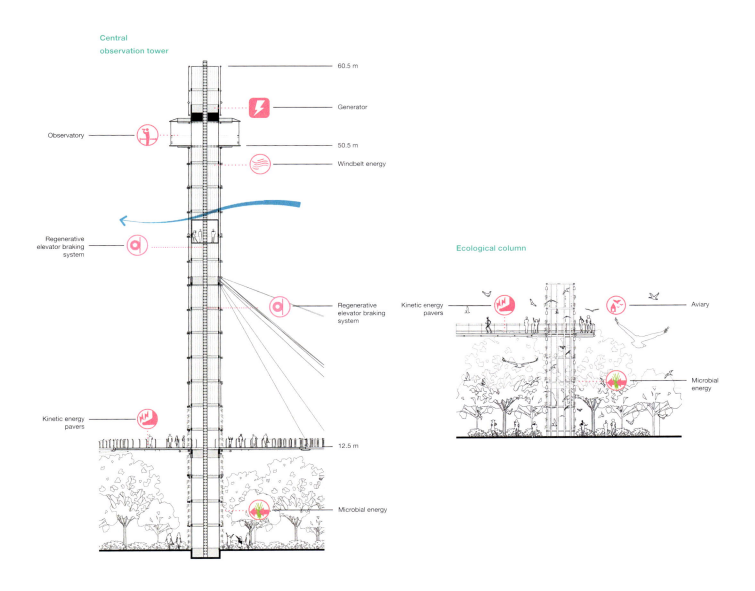

Night photosynthesis speeds up harvest times and maximizes quality and quantity during each harvest season. It combines the original light spectrum and the red spectrum to replace ultraviolet light at night.

The Flourishing Nest

DESIGNERS: Mohammad Reza Asgari, Osama AlSaab
ENERGY TECHNOLOGY: solar photovoltaic, vertical axis wind turbine (VAWT), droplet-based energy generator (DEG)
ANNUAL PRODUCTION: 7,000 MWh
OTHER SOCIAL CO-BENEFITS: stormwater harvesting, public library, meeting spaces, innovation lab, spaces for play and recreation

The Flourishing Nest is a place where people can come together in warmth and safety to learn from one another and celebrate life. Recognizing the importance of providing this kind of space within the city, the artwork is designed to blur the boundaries between humans and technology with the goal of increasing social and natural harmonies and leading us to a brighter future. It functions as a public park, school, and museum.

A structure comprising sustainably sourced wooden beams supports an undulating parametric form of solar modules. The artwork, located at the main crossroads of Spinelli Park, defines an inviting and open place for discovery and wonder, connecting people to the systems that power their lives.

The Flourishing Nest is designed as an aerodynamic shell, allowing cool air to flow unobstructed into the city. Some of the wind is harnessed with artful vertical axis wind turbine towers that define walking path junctures around the periphery of the installation and provide opportunities for park-goers to look out over the landscape from within the spinning frame.

The triangular photovoltaic modules provide geometrical flexibility in a modular form. Beneath each photovoltaic layer, a droplet-based energy generator (DEG) consists of polytetrafluoroethylene film on an indium tin oxide substrate with an aluminum electrode to generate electricity from the rain that strikes the surface of the module. Beneath the DEG, a transparent surface emits light with organic LEDs.

The Garden of Life is located in the center of *Nest* and is irrigated by stormwater harvested by the artwork and stored underground. The Garden is a place for the public to explore relationships between humans, nature, technology, and energy — a symbol of a society whose flourishing depends upon these factors. Within the shell surrounding the Garden, visitors will find a public library, a renewable energy innovation lab, quiet rooms, and spaces for play and recreation.

A new space called the Garden of Life is located in the center of the form—a symbol of the relationship between the four components of growth: human, nature, technology, and energy.

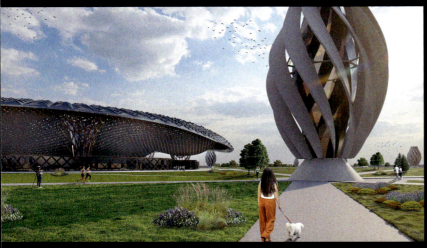

The vertical axis wind turbine towers act as wayfinding devices in the park.

The structure is made up of six different sections for public activities that include learning, play, recreation, food, commercial opportunities, and cultural events.

Floor plan

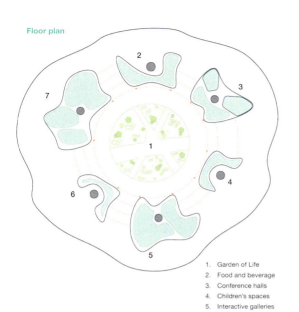

1. Garden of Life
2. Food and beverage
3. Conference halls
4. Children's spaces
5. Interactive galleries
6. Entertainment spaces
7. Library and bookstore

Site plan

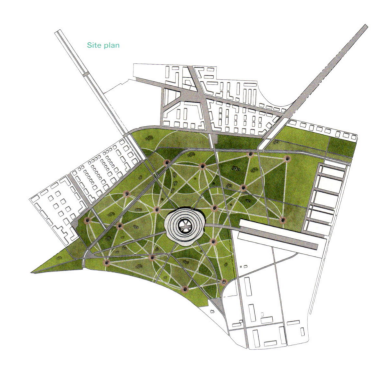

Exploded view

Solar panels

Wooden waffle structure

Circle grids, turbines, and pathways create different spaces across the site.

151

ma duneland

DESIGNERS: Jonas Eisenhofer, Daniel Klose, Jaira Pagkalinawan, Michelle Marker, Marie Hoffmann, Marlene Bögl, Jessica Messer, Esra Uyar

ENERGY TECHNOLOGY: algae bioreactors, thin-film solar photovoltaic, kinetic energy pavers

ANNUAL PRODUCTION: 280 MWh

OTHER SOCIAL CO-BENEFITS: research facility, educational workshops

From the bicycle to spaghetti ice cream, Mannheim has a long history of invention and innovation. Once touted for its sunny and warm climate, the city now faces overheating, climbing temperatures, and declining precipitation. Stale and polluted air, the heat, and other environmental problems impair the quality of life in Mannheim, leaving people in the city wanting a place where they can escape and recover.

ma duneland is a place for people of all ages to come together and connect. The fresh open greenspaces of Spinelli Park provide the perfect environment for work, leisure, and education. The land artwork is a retreat for humans and animals, a seamless, organic form that feels as if it has always been there. Mannheim's topographical location on a natural dune landscape gives rise to a microclimate that is home to a range of local flora and fauna. Due to its aerodynamic shape and low profile, the artwork supports the natural flow of air into the city.

Just as different people come together in *ma duneland*, the artwork also combines a variety of renewable energy sources. An algae bioreactor panel façade converts sunlight and carbon dioxide into renewable biofuel. The bioreactor façade also provides adaptive shading and acts as a thermal insulator. In addition, the dunes harness energy in the form of transparent thin-film solar panels artfully integrated as cladding on the southern side of the dunes. Heat insulating glass keeps interior temperatures comfortable and ideal for vertical gardening. A kinetic skatepark incorporates piezoelectric actuators within the paving surface to collect additional power from human energy.

Through its minimal touch on the landscape, *ma duneland* creates pockets of untouched green spaces and leaves nature to its own devices, giving it the chance to regenerate.

The *ma duneland* skatepark consists of a pump track that naturally fits into the landscape. As visitors use the skatepark, kinetic energy is collected and converted, allowing visitors to be an active part of the energy production.

ma duneland (continued)

The composition of forms in the landscape creates constellations of shapes and lines.

To educate people on the technologies used, the artwork includes Renewable Energy Lab Dunes. These are spaces within the naturally cool stone and clay walls where people can learn about the energy technologies incorporated into the installation and can make their own energy generating sculptures for their private gardens.

The outdoor and indoor area blur into each other.

Modular Innovation Cube

DESIGNERS: Elena Doht, Kai Beiderwellen, Ann-Kathrin Hauck, Lena Ackermann, Yehia Mallallah, Claudia Fratz, Theresia Schiller, Selina Ettinger, Madita Nisblé, Niklas Katz

ENERGY TECHNOLOGY: solar photovoltaic, micro wind turbines

ANNUAL PRODUCTION: 0.25 MWh per cube face (20–70 MWh per complete sculpture)

OTHER SOCIAL CO-BENEFITS: electronic device charging, air purification, CO_2 sequestration

Modular Innovation Cube (MIC) is a new medium for creating regenerative sculptural forms in public or private spaces. With its unique clickable attachment mechanism, the design offers an infinite range of attractive and sustainable options for Mannheim and its inhabitants. *Modular Innovation Cube* is a scaffolding for constant development, a stage for new technologies and innovations. It is designed for the present, for progress, and for the future!

The frame of each cube is a permanent component that accepts wall-element accessories that can be interchanged according to changing conditions. The most common accessory is a one-meter square photovoltaic module with an integrated micro inverter designed to work with its neighboring wall-elements to provide consolidated power for public use. The frame components can be fitted with single-axis tracking mechanics that are programmed to orient the solar accessory to the sun. Other wall-element accessories for the *MIC* sculptures include micro wind turbines and living moss panels to purify the air and sequester carbon.

The *Modular Innovation Cube* clickable attachment mechanism works with hinged flaps that can be locked open and closed with a key. This ensures the stability of the individual, high-quality wall-element accessories and makes the concept theft proof.

One example of the sculptural form is called the *MIC* Step, which represents the importance of boldly looking toward the future and imagining positive change. By taking this step, we shape new paths and dispense with older and unhelpful thought patterns. The generations who come after us should be able to experience this planet as a safe and thriving place. Through *MIC* Step and other sculptural forms composed with this new regenerative media, *Modular Innovation Cube* breathes new life into already familiar forms of renewable energy and makes them even more beautiful.

The *Modular Innovation Cube* system fits perfectly into the architectural structure and the theme of Mannheim—known as "Quadratestadt" (City of Squares).

The cubes rotate in their arranged rows and follow the sun's orientation during the day.

Modular Innovation Cube furniture in Spinelli Park.

Post-Terra

DESIGNERS: Jieun Yang, David Zhang, Rebecca Siqueiros (Habitat Workshop)
ENERGY TECHNOLOGY: dye-sensitized solar cells (DSSC) similar to Solaronix
ANNUAL PRODUCTION: 90 MWh
OTHER SOCIAL CO-BENEFITS: hydroponic urban farming, shaded gathering space

Responding to the current climate crisis — where droughts, flash floods, and heatwaves test the vulnerability of our infrastructure and ecosystems — *Post-Terra* reimagines the future of food security and energy production. It also highlights the intricate intertwining of the global supply chain, where an interconnected world makes us more reliant than ever on each other.

Hydroponic farming is often cited as a potential solution to future food scarcity. It uses up to 90% less land area and far less water than conventional methods. Typically grown in temperature-controlled indoor environments, seeds are planted in soil-free bio mediums, nutrients are fed via water to the plant roots sitting in a growth medium, and the sun is replaced with energy-intensive LED lighting. By bringing hydroponics outdoors — back to the sun and reconnected with nature — *Post-Terra* eliminates the high energy consumption of indoor vertical gardening and lowers its capital cost while maintaining its efficiencies and benefits.

The design creates an area of convergence at the intersection of two main paths through Spinelli Park and supports the objectives of the Climate Corridor (Klimopass), allowing fresh air to flow unobstructed into the city. The open-air structure is scalable from its minimum module to create a large green infrastructure.

Post-Terra recognizes the site's decades-long use as a military barracks and the potential lingering imperfections of the soil. As the name suggests, the project proposes an alternate form of crop production that reaches upward and integrates energy and sustainable social and economic production.

Clusters of hydroponic pavilion pods form the three concentric zones of social production: the market and agricultural center, the learning hub and community theater, and the play area and cooling center. Each pod is composed of four parts. The base contains a water reservoir, pump, and solar transformer. The middle contains rings of modular hydroponic pod trays made of food-grade stainless steel connected to drip pipes and the structural ring surrounding the center column. Above are pixelated solar rings using thin-film dye-sensitized solar cell (DSSC) technology. At the top, dew and fog collectors funnel water flow to reservoirs. Curtains for the upper-level pods and structural shading from above for lower-level pods help to offset extreme heat and cold, which makes outdoor hydroponics systems more vulnerable.

The clusters' layered and concentric growing pattern demonstrates a new model for future growth — an infrastructural seed planted for the future of Mannheim.

Visitors can participate with and wander through the market and agricultural center where agrivoltaics are utilized for symbiotic integrations of agricultural and solar energy production.

Post-Terra (continued)

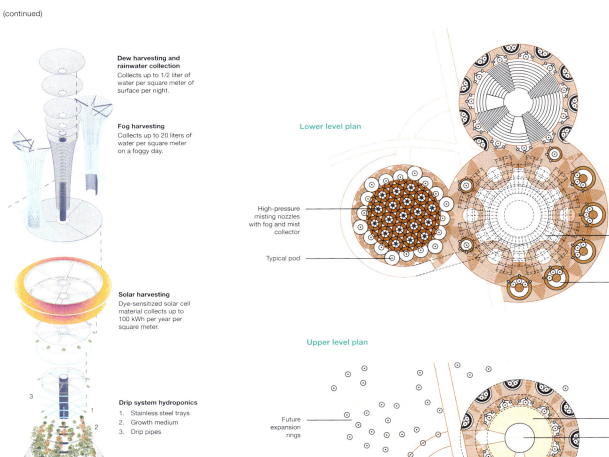

Dew harvesting and rainwater collection
Collects up to 1/2 liter of water per square meter of surface per night.

Fog harvesting
Collects up to 20 liters of water per square meter on a foggy day.

Solar harvesting
Dye-sensitized solar cell material collects up to 100 kWh per year per square meter.

Drip system hydroponics
1. Stainless steel trays
2. Growth medium
3. Drip pipes

Systems and storage
4. Water reservoir
5. Pump
6. Solar transformer

Lower level plan
- High-pressure misting nozzles with fog and mist collector
- Typical pod
- Dye-sensitized solar cell (DSSC) agrivoltaics
- Porous pavement

Upper level plan
- Future expansion rings
- Zone 3: Play area and cooling center, 52 m diameter
- Water reservoir and filtration
- General storage
- Zone 2: Learning hub and community theater, 48 m diameter
- Zone 1: Market and agricultural center, 72 m diameter
- PV battery storage

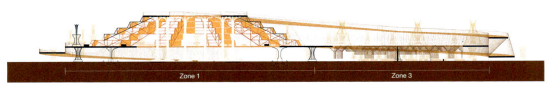

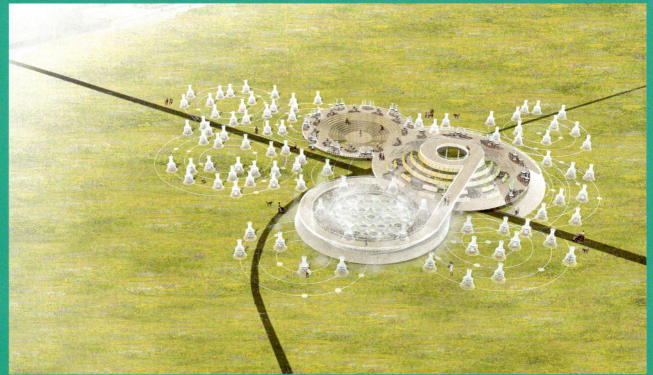

Post-Terra is composed of the following three concentric zones of social production working across multiple scales: market and agricultural center, learning hub and community theater, and play zone and cooling center.

treEcoTopia

DESIGNERS: Hannah Hammer, Gautham Thampy, Markus Schein, Mareike Schulte, Louisa Fiedler, Lea Seibel

ENERGY TECHNOLOGY: solar photovoltaic, vertical axis wind turbine

ANNUAL PRODUCTION: 5 MWh per large solar unit (up to 3,000 MWh across Spinelli Park)

OTHER SOCIAL CO-BENEFITS: 6 million liters of stormwater harvesting, playgrounds, exercise equipment, electronic device charging

treEcoTopia **is an artful energy landscape** that takes on a floral form and a forest-like composition, creating a human connection to energy production and the environment.

A forest of two types of modules spans across Spinelli Park, which are compatible with any masterplan and add to the beauty of the surroundings. Each *treEcoTopia* module is an independent vertical structure with a dedicated function. The first module type collects energy from the sun. A crown of stainless steel supports an array of solar panels oriented to face the sun. The second module type is designed to collect rainwater and early morning dew in a hydrophilic mesh. The supporting structures that comprise the trunk of each module are fabricated from corten steel and wood, and can include additional features, such as vertical axis wind turbines, lighting, and energy and water storage.

Both modules come in large and small sizes to create a dynamic composition throughout the park. Groupings of *treEcoTopia* modules are clustered to mimic the naturally occurring distribution of trees. Nearby playgrounds and exercise equipment are designed to generate additional clean energy from the movement of the swings, merry-go-rounds, seesaws, and stationary bicycles.

treEcoTopia (continued)

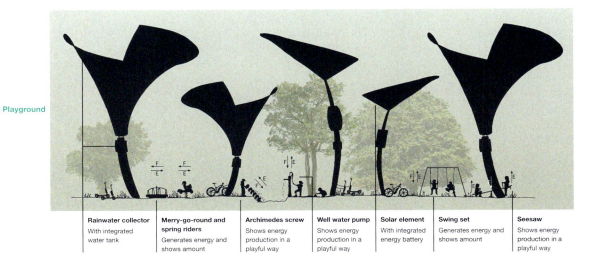

Playground

- **Rainwater collector** — With integrated water tank
- **Merry-go-round and spring riders** — Generates energy and shows amount
- **Archimedes screw** — Shows energy production in a playful way
- **Well water pump** — Shows energy production in a playful way
- **Solar element** — With integrated energy battery
- **Swing set** — Generates energy and shows amount
- **Seesaw** — Shows energy production in a playful way

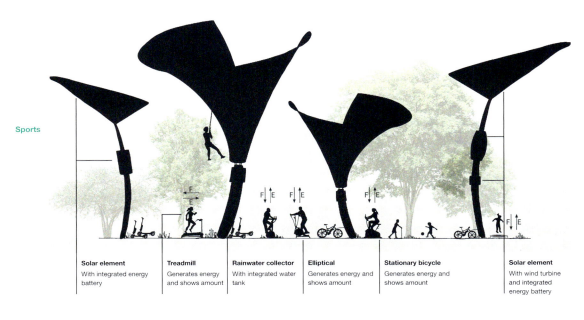

Sports

- **Solar element** — With integrated energy battery
- **Treadmill** — Generates energy and shows amount
- **Rainwater collector** — With integrated water tank
- **Elliptical** — Generates energy and shows amount
- **Stationary bicycle** — Generates energy and shows amount
- **Solar element** — With wind turbine and integrated energy battery

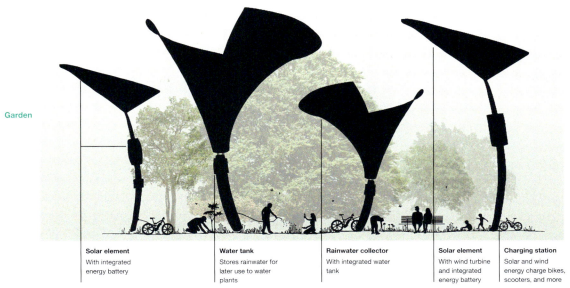

Garden

- **Solar element** — With integrated energy battery
- **Water tank** — Stores rainwater for later use to water plants
- **Rainwater collector** — With integrated water tank
- **Solar element** — With wind turbine and integrated energy battery
- **Charging station** — Solar and wind energy charge bikes, scooters, and more

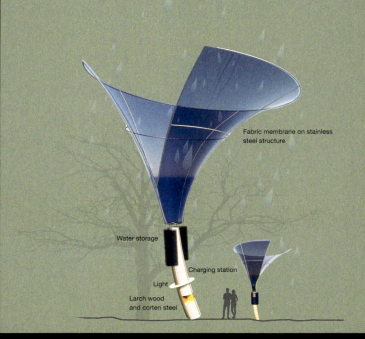

Water module components

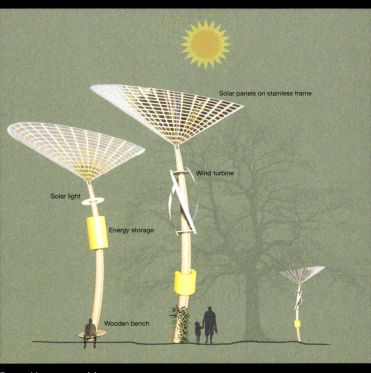

Renewable energy module

Cropergy: Essential Source of Life

DESIGNERS: Laura Borda, David Arismendis, Santiago Ardila, Andres Ibañez, Isabella Abril, Juan Diego León, Juan Bautista, Valerie Torres, Sofia Gaviria

ENERGY TECHNOLOGY: organic photovoltaic (OPV) solar, algae photobioreactor, microbial fuel cell (MFC)

ANNUAL PRODUCTION: 200 MWh

OTHER SOCIAL CO-BENEFITS: food for 4,700 households, CO_2 sequestration, greywater treatment, public space for gathering

Through a metabolic process of photosynthesis, plants synthesize food out of carbon dioxide, water, and sunlight. In a similar way, *Cropergy* harvests solar energy, water, and CO_2 in order to provide sustainable urban food crops.

The process begins with organic photovoltaic solar modules that convert sunlight into electricity. Some of that electricity is used to power an algae photobioreactor that cleans local greywater, while providing nutrients to vegetable gardens. Microbial fuel cells in the soil of the garden complete the cycle, producing additional electricity that provides ambient lighting at night.

Cropergy is composed of basic petal modules that allow plants to grow from the ground and climb up toward the sun. The modules are made of laminated timbers produced from renewable wood that can be grown rapidly within Spinelli Park. The structural components that make up the span of the petal alternate between algae bioreactor tubes and biopolymer pipes that supply an aeroponic cultivation system. The petal shape is inspired by the flower of a local, edible variety of Hemerocallis, commonly known as the daylily. Single petal modules can function as discrete pergolas or greenhouses, or they can be combined into larger functions. The stem grouping links up several petals to create pergolas along pedestrian walkways. The flower grouping links petals, radially giving rise to larger greenhouses and activity centers. A clear bioplastic manufactured from agricultural waste is used to enclose the greenhouses. Arrangements of petals are based on the local conditions, climate, and use of the park.

Pressures on agricultural production are increasing energy demand, water consumption, and land use. *Cropergy* is designed to grow the same quantity of food on one third less land area while consuming less water and energy. In addition to providing vegetables for more than a thousand area households, *Cropergy* achieves a net production of energy and purifies approximately two Olympic swimming pools of greywater volume each year. With *Cropergy*, existing parks can be turned into edible havens.

Cropergy: Essential Source of Life (continued)

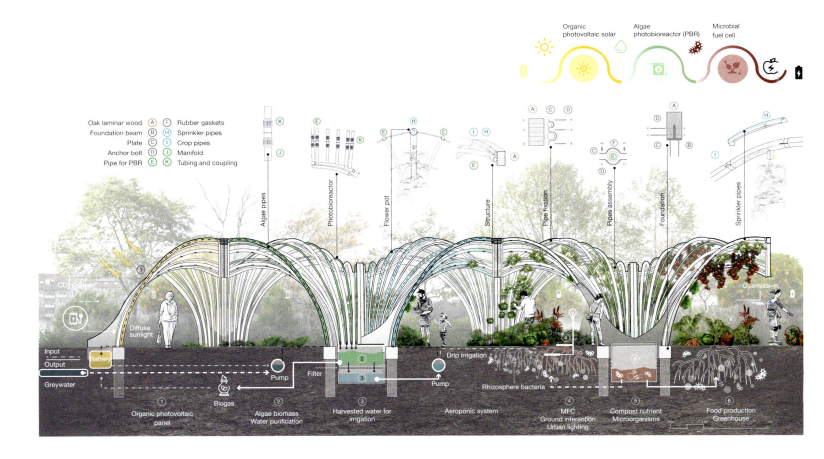

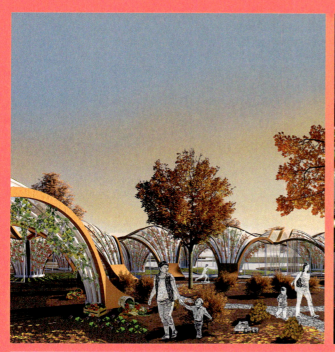

The artwork has plenty to offer park-goers throughout the seasons of the year.

The curving geometry of the artwork assists the function of the Climate Corridor—bringing fresh air to the Mannheim city center.

Hyperbolic Garden

DESIGNERS: Santiago Muros Cortés, Gabriele Mazza, Clara Cantarelo (GAMEPLAN Architects)
ENERGY TECHNOLOGY: solar photovoltaic
ANNUAL PRODUCTION: 112 MWh
OTHER SOCIAL CO-BENEFITS: food production, educational walking path, viewpoint

Hyperbolic Garden proposes a biomimetic approach to land and climate stewardship, one in which nature and humans become partners in a quest to restore balance and sustainability to our built environment. Within this paradigm, humanity does the designing and nature not only provides the building materials and techniques, but also the energy required to build and maintain new structures.

Inspired by the German Schrebergarten, the project produces sustainable, local, and naturally grown food through a 34-meter-tall vertical farm made from mycelium bricks. The hyperboloid shape protects fragile crops from excessive solar heat while maximizing sun exposure for crops with greater sunlight requirements. Crops are planted in the small gaps between bricks with roots hanging freely inside the core to maximize oxygen uptake. A constant water supply is maintained to each plant with a series of sprinkler rings that spray water from different heights. The sprinkler system inside the core and the cool microclimate created by the crops creates a ventilating stack effect and helps bring down the temperature of the air to contribute to the goals of the Climate Corridor.

Mycelium bricks are made from the root structure of fungus grown on a natural substrate, such as agricultural waste or sawdust. Their natural qualities make them an excellent option for constructing the core of the vertical farm. Not only do they sequester carbon in their creation, but they also have excellent hydrophobic, fire-resistant, and compressive properties. At the end of their useful life, they can be repurposed as fertilizer to continue to grow crops.

The mycelium brick core is reinforced from the inside by a locally harvested cross-laminated timber (CLT) substructure. Outside the core, a spiraling ramp provides access for visitors and stewards of the garden to plant and harvest the crops. This sculptural ramp also makes a fantastic observation platform for the newly developed Spinelli Park with phenomenal views all the way across the Neckar River. Surrounding the tower, an elevated walkway takes visitors on a tour of the UN Sustainable Development Goals.

Combining the innovations of vertical farming and agrivoltaics with biomimicry, revolutionary materials, and building techniques, *Hyperbolic Garden* is able to tackle multiple climate issues in a holistic and symbiotic way.

The ramp provides additional shading to the crops by acting as a brise soleil.

Hyperbolic Garden (continued)

Vertical farming is an efficient and sustainable way to produce high quality food in large quantities. Crops are stacked vertically, exponentially multiplying the productivity of a given plot of land and consuming up to 250 times less water than traditional farming. Because the crops are grown vertically with virtually no contact with soil, there are no pesticides or agrochemicals involved in the process.

The free-hanging roots can absorb as much water and oxygen as needed. Crops are typically grown in modular cylindrical towers made out of plastic that can be placed indoors or outdoors and are irrigated from within.

Fragile crops with less sunlight requirements are placed on the top half of the structure in a tangential position relative to the sun. Crops with higher sunlight requirements are placed at the bottom of the hyperboloid in a more perpendicular position relative to the sun.

Section diagram

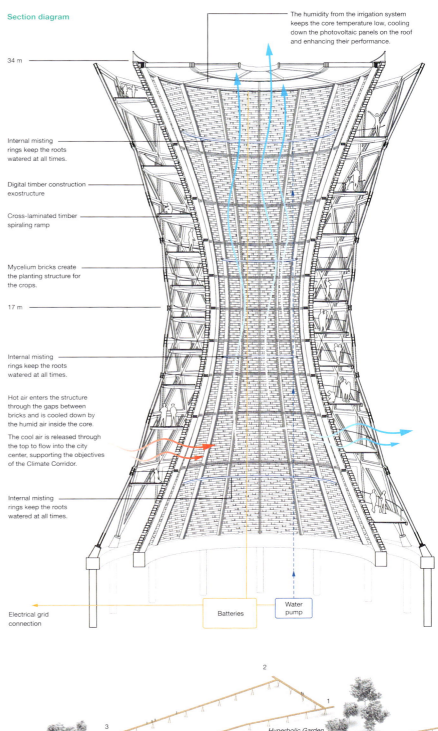

The humidity from the irrigation system keeps the core temperature low, cooling down the photovoltaic panels on the roof and enhancing their performance.

34 m

Internal misting rings keep the roots watered at all times.

Digital timber construction exostructure

Cross-laminated timber spiraling ramp

Mycelium bricks create the planting structure for the crops.

17 m

Internal misting rings keep the roots watered at all times.

Hot air enters the structure through the gaps between bricks and is cooled down by the humid air inside the core.

The cool air is released through the top to flow into the city center, supporting the objectives of the Climate Corridor.

Internal misting rings keep the roots watered at all times.

Electrical grid connection — Batteries — Water pump

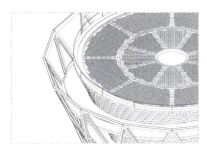

Monocrystalline photovoltaic panels on the roof of the structure power the artwork's lighting and hydroponic systems, and send excess energy to the city grid.

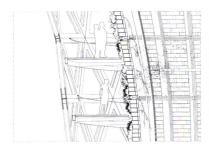

Crop roots hanging freely inside the core are watered by the misting system that maximizes the amount of oxygen and water absorbed by the crops, requiring far less water per pound of produce compared to conventional irrigation systems.

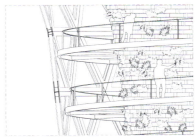

The core of the structure is built using mycelium bricks with gaps for planting crops. The ramp wraps around the core and provides access to tend the harvest.

Turn 1: SDG 2
End hunger, achieve food security and improved nutrition, and promote sustainable agriculture.

Turn 2: SDG 3
Ensure healthy lives and promote well being for all at all ages.

Turn 3: SDG 6
Ensure availability and sustainable management of water and sanitation for all.

Turn 4: SDG 7
Ensure access to affordable, reliable, sustainable, and modern energy for all.

Turn 5: SDG 9
Build resilient infrastructure, promote inclusive and sustainable industrialization, and foster innovation.

Turn 6: SDG 11
Make cities and human settlements inclusive, safe, resilient, and sustainable.

Turn 7: SDG 12
Ensure sustainable consumption and production patterns.

Turn 8: SDG 13
Take urgent action to combat climate change and its impacts.

The UN Sustainable Development Goals (SDGs) are directly addressed by *Hyperbolic Garden*.

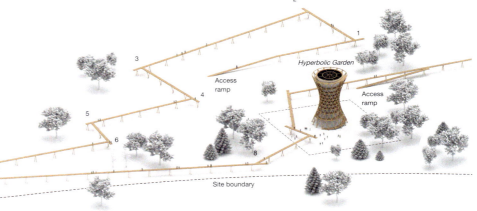

FEATURED ENTRIES

Power Nebh

Power Walk

The Dovecote & The Fallen Dovecote

Solar Leaf

The Solar Root

The Wave

Butterfly

Corridor of Life

In Time?

Knitted Orchards

Mannheim Murmurations

Poop, Play, Power

Room to Breathe

Spinelli Pillar

Square Roots

Tetravoltaics: Modular Tetrahedron Framework for Energy and Food Production

Flower Power: Forever in Bloom

Planktonic Synergy

The Energy+Art Garden

MOUND

Flower Farm

The Solar Poplars

Vibranergy: Energy Turned Into Vibrancy

Bloom: Purpose of Nature

Flower Garden

Walking in the Fields of Gold

Windwald

A Celebration of Light, Water, and Mirror

The Sun Flower

Eco-Art Pollinators

"Our ancestors considered light sacred and its source, the sun, life-giving. The brightness of the days began with the sunrise and ended with the sunset. For this reason, our ancestors often spoke of a battle between light and darkness, or between good and evil. They considered light as hope, life, and happiness, and darkness as the end, despair, and sorrow. At the beginning of each day, light wins over darkness and awakens hope."

— Shahed M. Yengiabad, Elaheh M. Yengiabad, and Alemeh M. Yengiabad

A Celebration of Light, Water, and Mirror

Power Nebh

DESIGNERS: María Guanumen, Andrés Ibañez, Juan Carlos Álvarez, Julián Escobar, Camila Segura, Alejandra Zamora, Natalia Sarmiento, Isabella Campos

ENERGY TECHNOLOGY: concentrated solar power (CSP) thermal generator

ANNUAL PRODUCTION: 30,000 MWh

OTHER SOCIAL CO-BENEFITS: air and water purification, public gathering space, interactive play

The steam engine gave birth to the Industrial Revolution, changing the technological paradigm of power generation and automating processes that were previously manual. To this day, most combustion engines are powered with carbon-based fuels and are responsible for the emission of vast amounts of carbon dioxide and other pollutants into the atmosphere, water, and soil.

What will be the future of steam energy in a post-carbon society? What if we could power a steam engine and generate electricity using the thermal energy of the sun while providing restorative benefits to the people and the environment? Could such a solution be a new work of art that enhances public space by evoking the city's industrial past?

Power Nebh uses concentrated solar power generation and transparent solar modules to generate electricity while cleaning stormwater and greywater from the Spinelli mixed use development and the park, greatly reducing downstream pollution. By evaporating water into the local environment, the artwork also helps to clean the air that flows across the site and into the city.

Power Nebh takes the dynamic form of clouds as a source of inspiration. Each of the 700 cloud modules in *Power Nebh* includes a parabolic trough CSP collector, a molten salt energy storage system, a 15 kW turbine, and a structure for capturing and releasing steam after it has been used to generate electricity.

A part of the steam is reintegrated into the system. Another part is retained by the textile surfaces, generating an immersive rain experience for visitors. The high temperatures and UV radiation make the resulting water suitable for plant irrigation. A small part of the steam is returned to the atmosphere as water vapor and reintegrated into the water cycle.

The cloud modules are arranged in groups of one to five, allowing various park activities at different scales. The release and collection devices offer shelter and shade by functioning as architectural canopies. These can be used for sports, community meetings, children's play, reading, and other activities. The areas of softly falling rain with its distinctive sound create an atmosphere that is fun, safe, and a comfortable place in which to play, connecting park-goers with the weather and the environment.

Power Nebh represents different types of clouds such as cumulonimbus, stratocumulus, altocumulus, cirrocumulus, and cirrus.

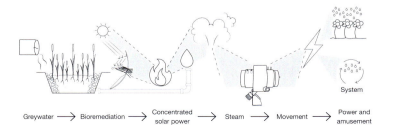

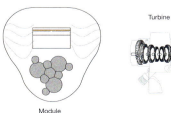

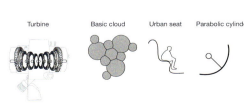

Components of the module

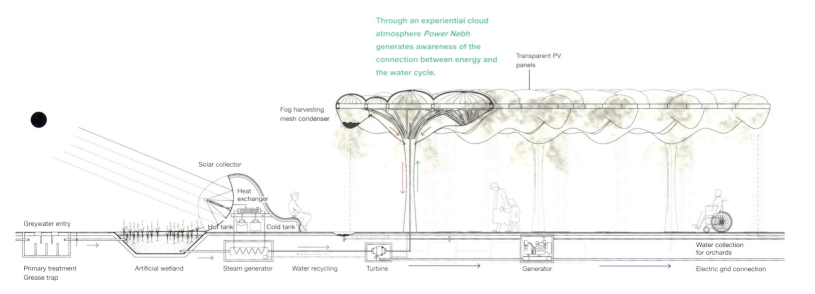

Through an experiential cloud atmosphere *Power Nebh* generates awareness of the connection between energy and the water cycle.

Power Walk

DESIGNERS: Abigail Barnes, Alyssa Hall, Nicholas Powell

ENERGY TECHNOLOGY: luminescent solar concentrator (LSC) photovoltaic

ANNUAL PRODUCTION: 4,000 MWh (4 MWh per module and 1,000 modules across the site)

OTHER SOCIAL CO-BENEFITS: shaded gathering space, public Wi-Fi, educational displays

Power Walk is a sculptural pedestrian experience that complements the innovative nature of Mannheim. Rather than a grand sculptural monument, the artwork is a simple creative gesture that could be implemented across a variety of site conditions. The design consists of modular canopies that transform pedestrian and bike pathways into inviting spaces that generate energy from solar radiation. By utilizing existing pedestrian and bike pathways, *Power Walk* preserves the maximum amount of green space within the site to allow for a versatility of uses.

Luminescent solar concentrator (LSC) modules create translucent sun shades that protect pedestrians from harmful solar radiation while also generating electricity to power amenities within the park and the surrounding neighborhood. The landscaping along the pathways includes a mix of native and edible plants providing habitat and food for native species and residents alike.

Power Walk can be as small as one modular unit for a private garden, or it can contain dozens of modules to cover stretches of pathways in a public park. The units can be arranged in several configurations including an arch, half arch, and butterfly design to maximize utility and aesthetics. At night, the structure becomes an inviting lighted walkway, connecting the surrounding areas of the city and providing safe meeting spaces. *Power Walk* paths serve not only as a means to get from one destination to another, but they are a destination in and of themselves.

Curious visitors to the park can learn about the solar technology incorporated into the artwork.

Subtle changes in the luminescence of the solar modules affects the patterns of light throughout the day. The rhythms of light within *Power Walk* change depending on if visitors are traveling through on foot or by bicycle.

The Dovecote & The Fallen Dovecote

DESIGNER: Mahyar Esmaili
ENERGY TECHNOLOGY: monocrystalline solar photovoltaic
ANNUAL PRODUCTION: 90 MWh
OTHER SOCIAL CO-BENEFITS: habitat for birds and animals

In the past, when human attention and respect for other living beings was more prevalent, entire buildings were dedicated to animals. A dovecote is a structure built for nesting birds. The traditional use of these buildings was to collect bird waste for use in agriculture before the industrial Haber-Bosch nitrogen production process was invented.

Humans have always been interested in birds. These beautiful creatures have become a symbol for peace and freedom. In addition to providing visual pleasure for humans, birds control the populations of insects and rodents that might otherwise do damage to agricultural fields and forests.

The Dovecote & The Fallen Dovecote respond to specific aims of the Spinelli Park plan to contribute to a thriving habitat for urban wildlife. The clay façade of the cylinder fits well within the urban agricultural context and provides an excellent climbing surface for plants and animals, such as the local wall lizard.

The roof plane measures approximately 70 m² and is clad with solar photovoltaic modules.

An integrated ladder allows easy access for maintenance of the structure and the solar power system.

The inner cylinder provides hundreds of square holes with suitable places for birds to nest. Birds can also roost on the structural beams that connect the inner and outer envelopes.

The outer cylinder envelope has perforations to allow birds to access roosting areas.

The ground plane becomes concave at the point where the artwork touches the ground.

Exploded axonometric diagram of the Dovecote structure

The Fallen Dovecote emerges from the landscape, providing habitat for local species. Its solar façade is oriented to capture midday sun.

The Fallen Dovecote has solar panels that generate electricity for more than 30 years and can be replaced with the solar technology of the 2060s.

Solar Leaf

DESIGNERS: Nuru Karim, Ayadi Mishra, Nirmal Kumar
ENERGY TECHNOLOGY: solar photovoltaic
ANNUAL PRODUCTION: 250 MWh
OTHER SOCIAL CO-BENEFITS: food production, public space for gathering and performance

Solar Leaf is a sustainable and interactive pavilion. Its space, structure, and skin are modular, adaptable, and scalable — designed to generate clean energy and produce healthy food within the same land area.

Solar panels with 50% transparency are arrayed across a structural timber framework made from sustainably sourced wood to create a sweeping form in the landscape and filter dappled sunlight into an open space below. The geometry is derived from the profile of a birch leaf, pinched and folded along its midrib and curving gently into the sky in a north-south orientation.

With the sides of the leaf facing east and west, the artwork generates electricity with two peaks — one in the morning and one in the evening, complementing the standard solar production curve that peaks once midday. The pavilion footprint measures 400 square meters — the same as the average German Schrebergarten — and varies in height from 3 meters to 12 meters. The system is adaptable and can be reconfigured to meet site constraints and energy requirements.

Solar Leaf can perform as a singular entity or as a cluster of solar leaves scattered across the site. Some exist as stand-alone solar pavilions with open space inside for gatherings and performances. Some include hydroponic gardens and greenhouses that thrive while requiring less irrigation water under the partial shade of the pavilion's solar roof. Still others may exist as greenhouses without solar modules for plants that require more sunlight.

Solar Leaf tells us the story of each leaf in a forest that contributes to the survival of the entire ecosystem. It's a story of hope and resilience in our collective effort to combat climate change and global warming.

A sequence of straight lines creates a complex curving form.

Hydroponics inside *Solar Leaf*

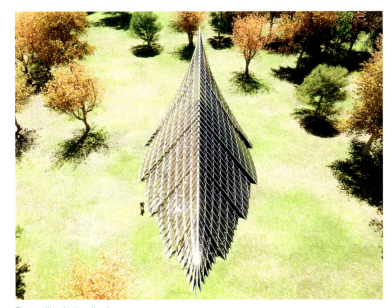

The pavilion is visualized as a self-sustainable system that harnesses solar energy and grows food.

Solar panels are proliferated across the structural timber harvested responsibly from well managed forests without

The Solar Root

DESIGNER: Kim Min Jae

ENERGY TECHNOLOGY: luminescent solar concentrator (LSC) photovoltaic

ANNUAL PRODUCTION: 1,350 MWh

OTHER SOCIAL CO-BENEFITS: gathering space for meditation

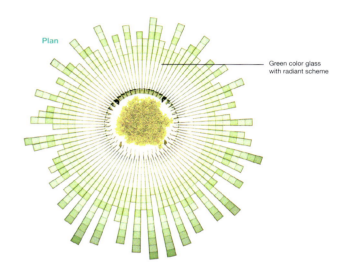

Trees have naturally formed a familiar relationship with humans throughout history. Large trees cast shade that becomes a recognizable place for gathering across generations. The tree also served as places of refuge from attacks by predators. Today, the importance of trees is again directly related to the survival of humankind although through a different set of important ecosystem services. Carbon emissions from human industrialization are colliding with an epidemic of deforestation to threaten the balance of the world's climate.

The Solar Root is a study on how to protect endangered trees while celebrating their centrality to human culture. A transparent wall of photovoltaic glass surrounds an endangered ginkgo tree at an important crossroads within Spinelli Park. At the foot of the wall is a public space for healing and reflection.

The Ginkgo biloba is one of the oldest living tree species in the world. Its striking yellow autumn leaf makes it an instantly recognizable symbol. The sole survivor of an ancient group of trees that date back to before the dinosaurs walked on Earth tens of millions of years ago, the ginkgo has an important place in human imagination. In his poem "Ginkgo biloba," Goethe praised the ginkgo leaf as a symbol of harmonious union between East and West.

The wall and floor panels that surround the tree are transparent solar photovoltaic glass luminescent solar concentrators (LSC). During the daytime, solar energy is converted into electrical energy and stored in batteries below the ground surface. Most of the produced electricity is fed into the grid through the "roots" of the artwork in the late afternoon when demand is at its peak, while some of the energy is used on site to create a captivating glow around the perimeter of the artwork throughout the night.

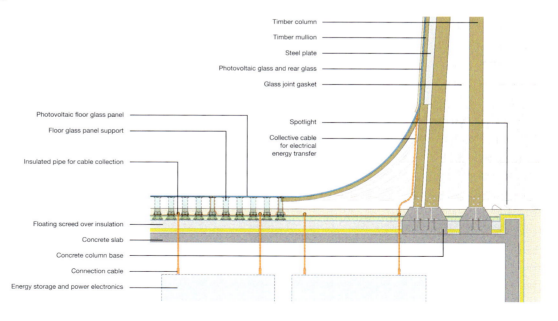

Each visitor to *The Solar Root* will form their own relationship to the tree at its center, which is protected in a way that pays homage to its regenerative nature.

The design of the protective wall is inspired by the roots and trunks of trees—making, storing, and distributing energy from sunlight.

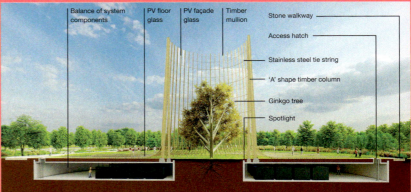

183

The Wave

DESIGNERS: Andre Enrico Cassettari Zanolla, Regiane Fernandes (Democratic Architects)

ENERGY TECHNOLOGY: luminescent solar concentrator (LSC) photovoltaic

ANNUAL PRODUCTION: 1,000 MWh

OTHER SOCIAL CO-BENEFITS: public space for gathering, crop production

The Wave is an interactive installation, a modular energy-generator, and an art piece designed to support the decarbonization goals of the City of Mannheim. Installed on top of the historic U-Halle building in Spinelli Park, the installation creates a new plane of experience, allowing visitors to walk through a technicolored sky tapestry of double-layered, energy-generating mesh.

The "floating" mesh is the main feature of the installation — a tensile network that is constantly reshaped by natural and human forces. The upper walking layer is made from highly resistant and nearly transparent steel mesh that is designed to withstand the weight of visitors. The system is inspired by the work of Berlin-based artist Tomás Saraceno (*In Orbit*, 2013), which has proven efficient, reliable, and replicable. The upper layer is interconnected with the lower luminescent solar concentrator (LSC) layer using tension and compression rods. When one layer moves, the other mimics its movement, maintaining a constant distance of 200 millimeters between the two. This distance is enough to avoid any obstructions in luminosity to the LSC panels but is still close enough so the upper mesh looks invisible to the visitors when seen from underneath.

The bottom layer is composed of a network of diamond-shaped LSC modules capable of producing electricity from direct and reflected light. Sunlight absorbed by LSC material is selectively refracted to the edges of the module where photovoltaic cells generate electricity from specific bands of energy. The wavelengths that are not refracted, including ultraviolet wavelengths, are re-emitted as visible light, giving the material a fluorescent quality. Subtle shifts in the wavelengths selected by the films in each module create a gradient spectrum across the installation. Each module is made from an organic-based bioplastic tile synthesized from vegetable waste.

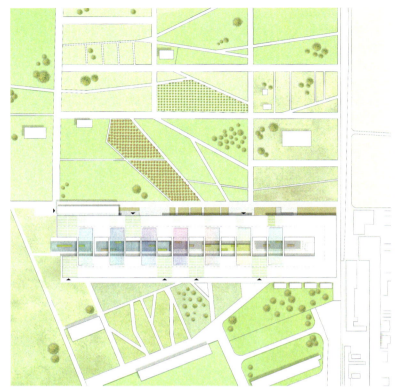

The selective transmission of colored light to the spaces below is used to stimulate photosynthesis as particular plants react differently to extended exposure to certain hues. This effect can enhance the color, flowering, fruiting, aroma, and flavor of the plants, and can increase the antioxidant content in their stems.

The red zone has ideal lighting for plants in flowering maturation.

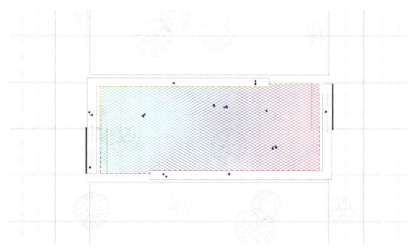

Accessible, nearly transparent steel mesh over LSC panels

The arrival experience includes shaded gardens over the entrance.

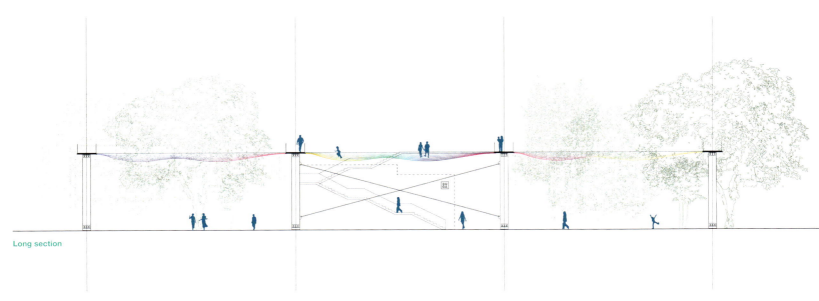

Long section

Butterfly

DESIGNER: Antonio Amézquita Zárate
ENERGY TECHNOLOGY: dye-sensitized solar cells (DSSC)
ANNUAL PRODUCTION: 28 MWh per unit
OTHER SOCIAL CO-BENEFITS: food production, shaded gathering space

A butterfly is intimately linked to the climatic cycles of the planet. Its diaphanous lightness and the harmony of its colors reflect nature's delicate balance.

Butterfly is versatile and adaptable, light and colorful, sustainable and friendly to the environment. It can be arranged both in civic spaces and in private gardens. As a closed shelter, the artwork offers protection from the elements and can act as a greenhouse. A manually operated cable and pulley mechanism opens two solar side panels in the manner of butterfly wings, transforming the artwork into an outdoor room or garden.

Butterfly can be used in large urban spaces, such as Spinelli Park, where two or more units can be arranged to form larger spaces. Single units can be installed in traditional German kleingärten.

The microclimates created by the wings of *Butterfly* extend growing seasons and the use of public spaces. The additional urban farming area helps to ensure food security and public health.

The low profile of the artwork integrates well with the objectives of the Climate Corridor (Klimopass), a component of the Baden-Württemberg climate adaptation plan intended to allow fresh air to flow unobstructed into the city. *Butterfly* demonstrates to the community aesthetic ways to fulfill sustainable planning objectives.

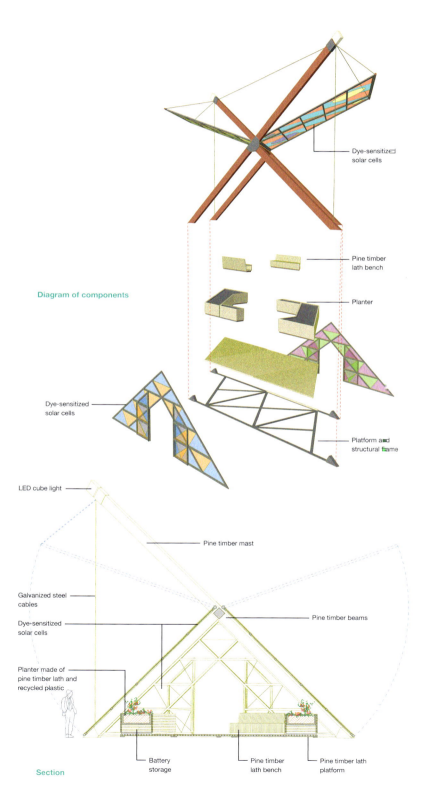

The solar panels can be folded down in the manner of butterfly wings through a manually operated cable and pulley mechanism.

Butterfly is adaptable and scalable for urban civic spaces and private gardens. The modular design allows it to be expanded by attaching two or more units under various arrangements.

Individual *Butterfly* modules can be placed end-to-end to create larger community gathering spaces and solar greenhouses.

The dye-sensitized solar cells create a magical interior of color and light much like the effect of stained glass windows.

Corridor of Life

DESIGNERS: Antonio Lamonarca, Olga Proshkina, Anqi Wang, Rhea Zouein, Gauri Prakash, Maria Madonnini

ENERGY TECHNOLOGY: compact acceleration wind turbine, dye-sensitized solar cell (DSSC) photovoltaic

ANNUAL PRODUCTION: 1,000 MWh

OTHER SOCIAL CO-BENEFITS: urban farming, shaded gathering spaces, migratory bird habitat

"The wisdom of nature is such that it produces nothing superfluous or useless but often produces many effects from one cause." — Nicolaus Copernicus

Corridor of Life takes inspiration and direction from the flows of nature. It is a permeable artistic sculpture modeled and engraved by the forces of the natural elements. The winds that flow through the park are channeled and accelerated to create electricity, while the energy of the sun is captured through installations of solar photovoltaic wings. Paths and walkways for the public meander around bodies of water that serve as stopover sites for migratory birds.

All of these elements form an energy generation landscape, where the sculptural beauty of the designed and natural elements coexists in harmony across multiple scales.

Compact acceleration wind sculptures channel moving air that passes at its greatest velocity across turbines positioned in the narrow part of the concentrator. The curving form of the wind concentrators create amphitheaters for large events that are powered by the energy produced. Other concentrators power spaces for sports, leisure activities, and exhibitions.

In addition to wind generated energy, "solar wings" follow the physical and energetic paths of the sun. Set above the ground five to seven meters, the wings provide shade and define diverse and multifunctional spaces underneath. These sculptures, designed to imitate the passage and migration of birds, are clad on their top surface with semi-transparent, dye-sensitized solar cells and provide protection for gathering spaces and community gardens below.

The upper part of the installation is made with semi-transparent dye-sensitized solar cells, supported by a light recycled metal structure, giving pleasant shade on a sunny day to people underneath. Public seating, water features, and planted areas are integrated into the design of the ground plane below.

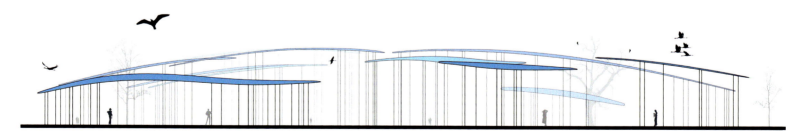

Elevation view of the solar elements, which float above like wisps of cloud, freeing the ground plane for park use and allowing the flow of fresh air into the city.

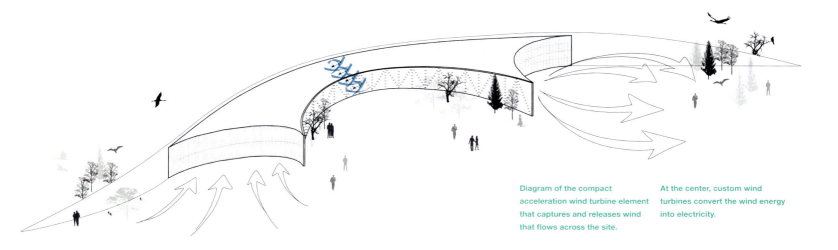

Diagram of the compact acceleration wind turbine element that captures and releases wind that flows across the site.

At the center, custom wind turbines convert the wind energy into electricity.

Park-goers and waterfowl enjoy the engineered wetlands that purify water using the natural treatment technique of phytodepuration.

View from above

In Time?

DESIGNER: Aditya Mandlik
ENERGY TECHNOLOGY: multi-junction solar photovoltaic
ANNUAL PRODUCTION: 600 MWh
OTHER SOCIAL CO-BENEFITS: food production, shaded gathering space, water harvesting

Climate change is a gradual and unseen process for many. However, the stories from those whose lives are forever changed by floods, fires, droughts, and storms are tragic. For them the change is very visible. How can we impart a sense of urgency through a work of art in public space?

In Time? is a giant clock for the City of Mannheim, ticking away toward a sustainable future. The artwork is positioned at a crossroad of walkways, biking paths, and the decommissioned rail line.

Seven pie-shaped public spaces each represent a day of the week. Twenty-four columns within each section represent the hours of a day. As the day begins, all twenty-four columns have their LED lights turned off. Similar to the hands of a clock, one additional column lights up as each hour passes, symbolizing the urgency of the climate crisis.

Beneath the columns, landscape compositions encourage play and creativity while creating a variety of outdoor rooms and social experiences. Each of the 168 columns is a metabolic element, composed from the top down of light cones, solar fins, horticulture pods, vertical gardens, energy storage, and water-harvesting cisterns. The solar fins are programmed to optimize solar collection, and each column is scaled in proportion to its location within the larger arrangement.

The horticulture pod is designed to nurture saplings within the shaded environment using filtered stormwater and greywater. As the saplings grow, they provide fresh air while surrounding park-goers with greenery. When they are mature, they are rotated out and planted in the surrounding park. About 40% of the energy generated by the solar canopy is used to support the horticulture pods, irrigation, site lighting, public charging, and other local functions, while 60% of the electricity is sent back into the city's grid.

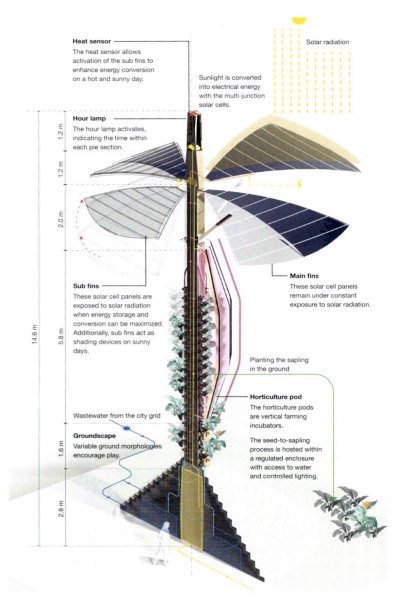

Section drawing expressing the dynamic morphology of the changing ground. Various use cases are activated within the same spaces, which can be rearranged and adapted.

Spatial transition between two of the seven public spaces

Interior view of Pie 1 showing the jogging track with stepped sides that allow multiple uses.

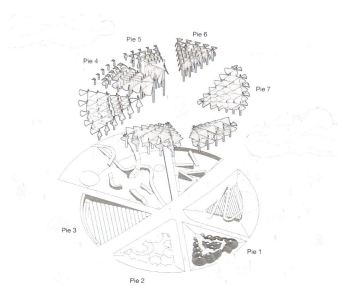

Axonometric view showcasing seven different ground morphologies that enhance creative engagement of the space with its users.

Knitted Orchards

DESIGNERS: Luis Gutierrez, Aram Badr, Andrei Stan
ENERGY TECHNOLOGY: solar photovoltaic fabric
ANNUAL PRODUCTION: 20 MWh
OTHER SOCIAL CO-BENEFITS: exercise, gardening, water harvesting, public space for gathering, personal electronic device charging

Knitted Orchards is a public greenhouse where visitors to Spinelli Park learn about horticulture and sustainable energy in a fun and engaging environment. The structure is composed of bright, curving fabric planes that provide hanging planting beds for local vegetables, fruits, and flowers along with spaces for gathering and for creative installations.

Courageous visitors will take advantage of the areas designed for climbing to take in a fresh perspective on the park. Above them the curving forms of the artwork integrate a solar photovoltaic fabric mesh within the top sections that generates energy for the park and the surrounding city. The entire mesh of *Knitted Orchards* is designed to harvest atmospheric water from early morning dew condensation, which collects and meanders down to the planting areas at the ground level.

The hyperbolic geometry of *Knitted Orchards* is modular. Each unit is composed of twelve identical quarter arcs that allow additional units to be added to an original installation over time. Versions with fewer quarter arcs can also be used in private gardens. Its thin and aerodynamic form allows the wind to flow freely in and around the artwork to support Spinelli Park's role in the Climate Corridor that brings fresh air into the city center. The folding geometry allows for thin structural piping that supports the stretched knitted mesh material, which is made from high-strength polyester yarn designed to withstand the weather and seasons of Mannheim.

The selected crops are a combination of water-purifying and fruit-producing plants that are typically found in the area of Baden-Württemberg. Plants are placed in accordance with their function, water needs, and growth style in order to increase their efficiency. Herbs that filter the water are placed on top of the structure followed by the fruit and vegetable crops below.

The solar fabric is woven with electronic yarn created by embedding small crystalline silicon solar cells connected with copper wires within the fibers of a textile yarn. Energy is stored in batteries situated in the interior of the structure, creating an artwork that serves as charging stations for devices ranging from mobile phones to electric scooters.

The structure provides community areas where the transparency and the surrounding vegetation creates space for programming.

Section showing the connection of twelve modules

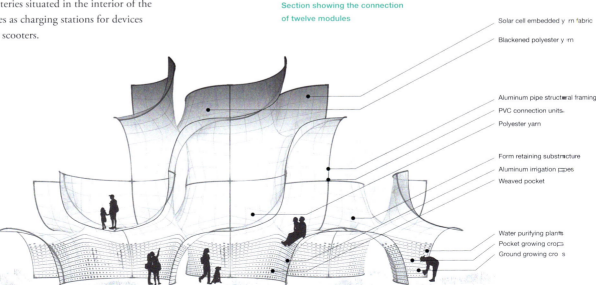

Solar cell embedded yarn fabric
Blackened polyester yarn
Aluminum pipe structural framing
PVC connection units
Polyester yarn
Form retaining substructure
Aluminum irrigation pipes
Weaved pocket
Water purifying plants
Pocket growing crops
Ground growing crops

Neighbors tend and harvest the vertical gardens.

Small version for a kleingarten

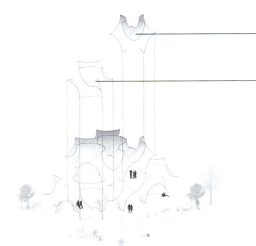

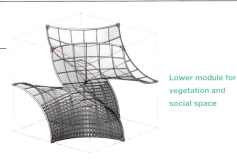

Lower module for vegetation and social space

Upper module for solar and water collection

193

Mannheim Murmurations

DESIGNERS: Peter Coombe, Jennifer Sage, Lee Kuhn, Charlotte Sie Wing Ho, Max St. Pierre, Kelsey Cohen, Annabel Coleman, Michael Piderit, Antonia Januzzi-Thomas, Caitlin Watson, Kit Yan, Harry Hooper, Claudia Chang

ENERGY TECHNOLOGY: organic photovoltaic solar cells

ANNUAL PRODUCTION: 100 MWh

OTHER SOCIAL CO-BENEFITS: pollination, habitat restoration, research

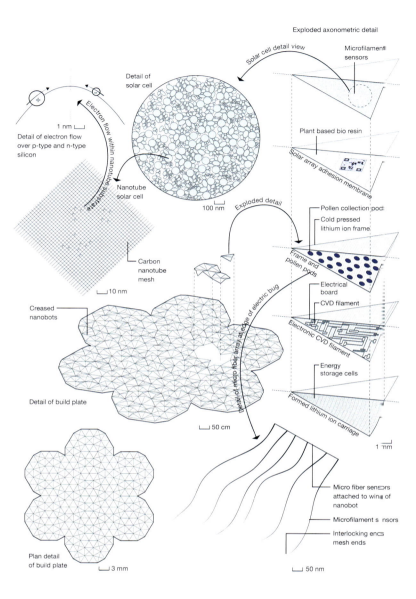

Mannheim Murmurations celebrates the startling advances in nano and robotic technology, suggesting an alternate scale of green energy production that is not tied to the twentieth century model of centralization. Rather, it demonstrates how living systems can co-exist and be supported by populations of biomimetic nano-modular assemblies. These nanobots are temporary guardians and docents for fragile biological communities.

Local pollinator habitats are under attack and many pollinators, including butterflies, moths, bees, and bats, are on the verge of collapse. Without natural pollinators, the future of all reliable human food supplies is in peril.

The robotic *Murmurations* do the work of the decimated insect pollinators, nurturing insects and indigenous plant communities until the natural ecosystems can be restored. From there, these robotic species will migrate (under their own photovoltaic power) to support other threatened biological systems throughout Germany or will be deconstructed and recycled at a processing facility within the U-Halle.

The nanobots are programmed or tasked with activities normally carried out by the indigenous insect populations, such as pollination and warding off invasive species. Other combinations of bots assist naturalists, biologists, and park-goers. The primary function of the bots is energy collection, storage, and distribution. Always ready to help, you may see bots recharge a mobile phone or two, or gather together to charge an electric scooter or bicycle. The bots are an ever-migrating photovoltaic array, ready to create and distribute power wherever and whenever needed.

The nanobots are produced by composite-carbon three-dimensional printers as sophisticated multi-layered sheets incorporating high-density battery storage, nanocircuitry for controls, microfiber sensors, and ultra-thin organic photovoltaic cells produced using a novel tetraphenyldibenzoperiflanthene (DBP) vapor deposition process.

The sheets are composed of tiled triangular modules, which are laser cut to produce a variety of nanobot units. The patterning allows the robots to micro-crease, become rigid, and actuate for flight over a medial folding axis. Once mobile, these various units can self-assemble into larger structures, each designed to fulfill a specific role.

Production and repair facility

Mannheim Murmurations proposes flying nano-robots as temporary guardians and docents for fragile biological communities.

Mono Di Tri Tetra Penta Hexa Hepta Octa Ennea Deca Hendeca Dodeca Triskaideka

Each type of nanobot unit has a specialized function and performs different regenerative tasks around Spinelli Park. The Mono, the most basic unit, pollinates and seeks to combine with other units to perform specific tasks. Each Mono will generate one watt-hour of electricity per year. Tri units are weeders and help control invasive species. Tetra units are pollinators, assisting the bees and hummingbirds. Penta germinating units plant seeds for future growth. Hexa units are capable of finding broken units of other types and coming to their rescue. Hepta units perform real-time monitoring of the weather conditions of microclimates. Octa units act as human interfaces, assisting visitors with wayfinding, translation, and species identification. Other units include the Triskaideka, the largest unit, which provides charging.

Poop, Play, Power

DESIGNERS: Haoran Wang, Joie Chan
ENERGY TECHNOLOGY: biogas from anaerobic digestion, kinetic energy pavers
ANNUAL PRODUCTION: 300 MWh
OTHER SOCIAL CO-BENEFITS: public toilets, waste disposal, playground

As the amount of waste increases, methane gas slowly inflates the dome.

As much as we love our fur babies, we must admit dog poop causes serious environmental issues. Besides its unpleasant sight and smell, harmful pathogens can be found in dog poop and, when it is left uncollected, it becomes a source of water pollution. Some pet parents may argue that they have done their part in protecting the environment by picking up after their pets. Although it may have helped prevent the dog waste getting washed directly into a local waterway, all those plastic bags that go into a trash bin will eventually end up in a landfill and will contribute to methane gas in the atmosphere, which is a more potent greenhouse gas than CO_2.

Poop, Play, Power! combines a dog park, a restroom with a waste digestion structure, and a playground to generate renewable energy. It collects all dog waste from the new development along the north of Spinelli Park, as well as biodegradable household waste and human waste from park visitors and transforms this unwanted mass into renewable energy using anaerobic digesters. Additional energy generated from kinetic energy harvesting in the playground area is used to power the anaerobic digestion process.

The biogas is stored in the dome above the public restroom. The dome is made from an elastomeric material and is reinforced with synthetic fabrics for high tensile strength and abrasion resistance. The volume of biogas generated is made visible by the inflation of the dome, which rises as more gas is produced. At night, the dome is lit up and becomes a screen for artwork projections.

There are three end products from the biodigestion process: biogas, liquid fertilizer, and solid remains. A generator connected to the digester transforms biogas into electricity to power park lights, light shows, and other park features. A portion of the electricity is stored in batteries and the balance is fed to the grid to help power nearby households. After proper sanitization, the liquid fertilizer can be used to fertilize landscaped areas of the park or given away to kleingarten owners. The solid remains are buried throughout the park creating land arts of different shapes and sizes over time.

The artwork transforms current perspectives on poop as a problem to poop as a solution and a resource. *Poop, Play, Power!* is a placemaking solution that generates renewable energy while creating a space to foster community and educate the next generation about energy consumption.

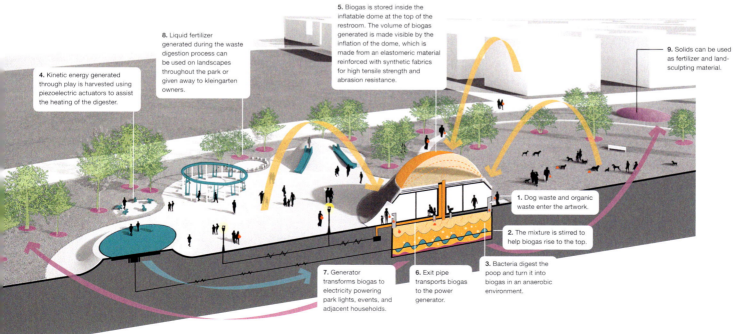

4. Kinetic energy generated through play is harvested using piezoelectric actuators to assist the heating of the digester.

8. Liquid fertilizer generated during the waste digestion process can be used on landscapes throughout the park or given away to kleingarten owners.

5. Biogas is stored inside the inflatable dome at the top of the restroom. The volume of biogas generated is made visible by the inflation of the dome, which is made from an elastomeric material reinforced with synthetic fabrics for high tensile strength and abrasion resistance.

9. Solids can be used as fertilizer and land-sculpting material.

1. Dog waste and organic waste enter the artwork.

2. The mixture is stirred to help biogas rise to the top.

7. Generator transforms biogas to electricity powering park lights, events, and adjacent households.

6. Exit pipe transports biogas to the power generator.

3. Bacteria digest the poop and turn it into biogas in an anaerobic environment.

197

Room to Breathe

DESIGNERS: Tom Esdar, Maximilian Bohnhorst, Hamed Samara
ENERGY TECHNOLOGY: Windbelt™ (aerostatic flutter
ANNUAL PRODUCTION: 1,500 MWh
OTHER SOCIAL CO-BENEFITS: personal electronic device charging, partly shaded gathering spaces

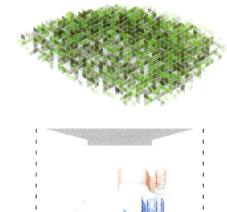

As cool air flows from the wooded hills to the northeast gently through the Rhine-Neckar Climate Corridor and across Spinelli Park on its way into Mannheim, it has an extra role to play in the sustainable life of the city. Windbelt screens create outdoor rooms and add a splash of color and energy as they vibrate in the gentle breeze.

The screens incorporate a novel type of wind energy generation technology, the Windbelt developed by inventor Shawn Frayn. Windbelts use the physics of aerostatic flutter to generate electricity. As the wind flows across a thin stretched membrane, it causes the membrane to vibrate. Magnets located at the two ends of the membrane move between copper coils as they flutter from the vibration and generate an alternating electrical current (AC power) as a consequence of Lenz's law of self-induction.

From a distance the artwork appears reminiscent of a green hill, a conceptual extension of the wooded topography to the north — a visual connection to the Climate Corridor. While tall and wide, the structure is very light and appears almost as a Fata Morgana as the vibrating belts blur the perception of the landscape beyond.

Room to Breathe makes the invisible wind an element that can be experienced with all human senses. Like any vibrating body, the membranes emit a sound which is perceived by visitors and accompanies them during their discoveries. In the center of the pavilion, gathering spaces include hammocks where visitors can feel the wind on their skin in the semi-shade of the screens.

Maze-like walls and tubes create a sound experience.

The core is a space for relaxing and feeling.

Elevation

Night perspective

Spinelli Pillar

DESIGNERS: Charles Ye, Cindy Zhang, Frank Yan, Ge Qian, Jonathan Chang, Leo Wang, Sue Qin, Victor Lo, Yifei Lou, Zoe Zhang

ENERGY TECHNOLOGY: luminescent solar concentrator (LSC) photovoltaic

ANNUAL PRODUCTION: 1,000 MWh

OTHER SOCIAL CO-BENEFITS: wayfinding landmark, urban food production

Spinelli Pillar is an energy-generating landmark anchored within the Climate Corridor of Mannheim. The tower is both a tribute to the past and a promise to the future.

Rising from the center of the new Spinelli Park, the artwork pays homage to the selfless actions of the site's namesake, U.S. Private First Class Dominic V. Spinelli, who sacrificed his own life to save the lives of others. It is also a reminder of the collective bravery and courage required to overcome the challenges of our past while working together for a brighter future.

The simple form draws attention to its lattice-like façade, inspired by the small garden trellises used to support plants, and is composed of luminescent solar concentrator photovoltaic (LSC) panels and vertical living walls. The LSC panels generate electricity within a semi-transparent glass pane. They do this with a special light-scattering luminescent layer within the glass that refracts certain wavelengths of light to the edges of the panel where they are collected by photovoltaic cells. The conversion efficiency — less than half that of conventional solar modules — is more than outweighed by the beauty of the material. At night the tower can be seen from a distance, its organic luminescent dyes creating a glow of soft oranges, yellows, and reds while the LSC panels continue to harness electricity even from the artificial light within.

Visitors to the structure will enjoy select viewpoints of the surrounding park and the City of Mannheim. Those who can are encouraged to make the climb all the way to the top — a symbolic journey representing the challenge and hard work entailed by the transition from a carbon economy to one powered by clean energy.

Around the base of the tower, the monumental transforms into the pedestrian. A colorful, self-sufficient streetlamp generates electricity throughout the day and illuminates the street at night. A modular gardening trellis provides power for irrigation and personal electronic devices. These smaller elements quickly spring up in the streets and private gardens of Mannheim, extending *Spinelli Pillar* into the community.

Obelisk   Lamp   Trellis

At the pedestrian level, the landmark transforms to an elegant self-sufficient streetlamp, where the energy generated by LSC panels during the day illuminates the street at night.

The streetlamps, arrayed toward *Spinelli Pillar*, provide a wayfinding path to the main obelisk — reminding us of the possibilities of clean energy.

Immediately entering the structure, one is met with stairs that spiral to the top. Along the way visitors are given select viewpoints of the City of Mannheim. The grand panoramic vista is offered to those who finish the hike. A slow elevator ride down to the ground floor offers a moment to cool down.

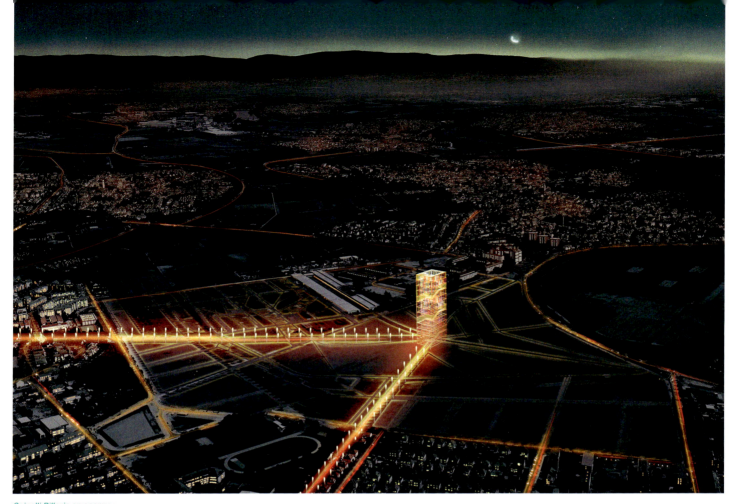

Spinelli Pillar is an energy-generating landmark anchored in the Climate Corridor of Mannheim.

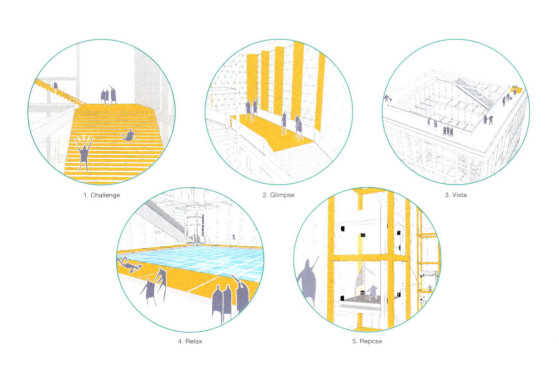

1. Challenge
2. Glimpse
3. Vista
4. Relax
5. Repose

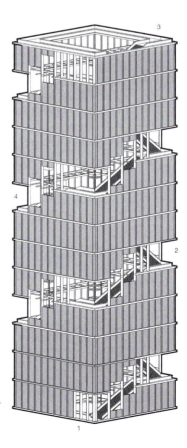

Square Roots

DESIGNER: Riccardo Mariano

ENERGY TECHNOLOGY: monocrystalline solar photovoltaic

ANNUAL PRODUCTION: up to 4 MWh per module (16,000 MWh if installed across the entire park)

OTHER SOCIAL CO-BENEFITS: public space for gathering, crop production

Square Roots is a modular sculpture inspired by the common shape of the fundamental unitary component of a photovoltaic system — the solar cell. The form of the artwork module is reminiscent of the archetypal shape of a house as drawn by young children. This deceptively simple iconic form is the building block for a three-dimensional grid at civic-park scale in Mannheim. The arrangement of modules of four different sizes turns the very rational configuration of the single element into an organic pattern inspired by fractals and repeating patterns found in nature.

The variety of scales and configurations allows for different public activities including community gardens, agrivoltaic fields, greenhouses, aviaries, animal shelters, huts, and sheds for tools. Each one produces clean electricity while fulfilling its social benefit.

There are two versions of the module at each of the four scales. The south-facing module allows for more density within an array and features a slightly better sun exposure. The east-west-facing module provides twice the area of solar panels oriented to provide energy in the morning and late evening to complement the south-facing module's midday peak.

With a low elevation and a light footprint on the landscape, *Square Roots* allows the ground plane and people to flow continuously below while the wind flows unimpeded above.

Different programs

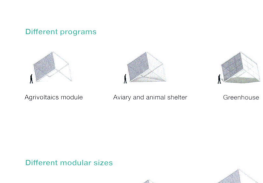

Agrivoltaics module | Aviary and animal shelter | Greenhouse | Hut

Different modular sizes

1.5 m side
Cold frame

5 m side
Agrivoltaics module, small greenhouse, or tool shed

10 m side
Agrivoltaics module, medium greenhouse, aviary, or animal shelter

15 m side
Agrivoltaics module, large greenhouse, aviary, or animal shelter

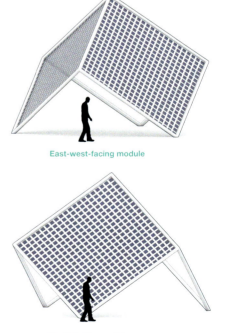

East-west-facing module

South-facing module

The different modular sizes of *Square Roots* create a variety of outdoor rooms to explore throughout the park. Each module touches the ground lightly in only three places, leaving the landscape relatively undisturbed.

The repeating modules strike the perfect balance between cost efficiency and aesthetic quality of space. Frequent visitors to Spinelli Park will discover their favorite hidden corners to return to time and again.

A square is the most efficient form on which to array solar cells.

A cube is a made from six squares and is the minimal sculptural form.

A rotated cube is oriented for optimal photovoltaic energy production and rainwater collection.

A structure traces the rotated cube with a flexible skeletal frame.

Photovoltaic cells are integrated on one or two faces.

Shape development diagram of individual module

A dynamic and engaging solar energy landscape emerges in Spinelli Park—an iconic symbol of sustainability for the City of Mannheim.

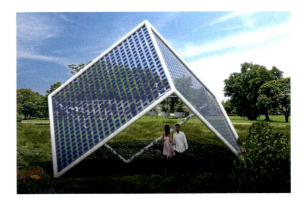

Tetravoltaics: Modular Tetrahedron Framework for Energy and Food Production

DESIGNERS: Daekwon Park, Angelina Yihan Zhang, Chenhao Luo, Nicholas Chung

ENERGY TECHNOLOGY: organic photovoltaic (OPV) solar

ANNUAL PRODUCTION: 10,000 MWh

OTHER SOCIAL CO-BENEFITS: food production, playgrounds, sports and recreation spaces, rainwater harvesting

The structures are made from sustainable materials and are designed and manufactured using computational design and digital fabrication techniques.

Within Spinelli Park, the gateway to the Rhine-Neckar Climate Corridor, three distinctive smaller parks — the Community Park, the Garden Park, and the Solar Park — engage with the ecological landscape to the south and the residential and commercial neighborhoods to the north. The Community Park provides amenities for people, the Garden Park provides food and natural beauty, and the Solar Park provides energy and water.

Tetravoltaics is an homage to Mannheim's spirit of innovation in urban planning and mobility. Inspired by Mannheim's grid-patterned city center, each of the three parks are connected with creative walking and biking paths.

The tetrahedral lattice modules of *Tetravoltaics* can be assembled into various configurations, forms, and scales. As a modular design system, the application can range from furniture scale (bench, planter, streetlight) to architecture and landscape scales (viewpoint, greenhouse, aeroponic tower, rest pavilion, playground, irrigation system, and bridge).

In the Solar Park, a field of sail structures within large open areas harvest solar energy, collect rainwater, and provide shade to visitors. In the Garden Park, the modular farming system uses the hollow core tetrahedron modules to circulate water through greenhouses and aeroponic planters. The Community Park is home to playgrounds, sports and recreation spaces, rest stations, and art installations that foster a healthy lifestyle for visitors of all ages. The network of bicycle and pedestrian walkways extends from these spaces throughout the site and beyond to further encourage active living.

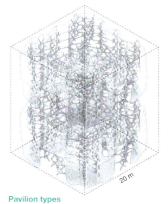

Pavilion types

Pavilion A is a greenhouse structure located in the Solar Park, which consists of large open areas and lawns where fields of sail structures harvest solar energy, collect rainwater, and provide shade to visitors.

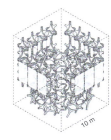

Pavilion B is an observatory structure located in the Garden Park, which utilizes a productive landscape design that integrates food production with the public park. Vegetables, herbs, and flowers are grown using various methods, such as raised beds, greenhouses, and aeroponic towers.

Pavilion C is a dispensary structure located in the Community Park which provides amenities including playgrounds, sports, recreation spaces, rest stations, and art installations.

Solar Park

Garden Park

Community Park

Modular energy harvesting system

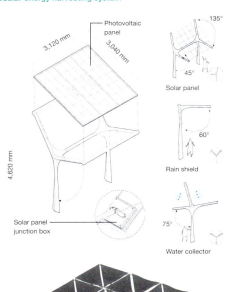

Tetravoltaics utilizes thin-film organic photovoltaic (OPV) membranes.

Modular aeroponic farming system

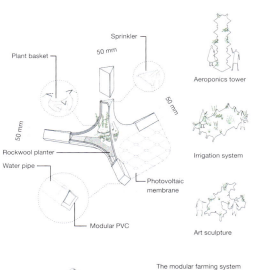

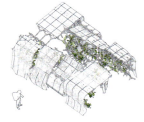

The modular farming system is a series of structures that support and foster food production. A network of embedded water pipes and low pressure pumps within the hollow core tetrahedron modules circulate, filter, store, and distribute water through the assembly to irrigation systems, greenhouses, and aeroponic systems.

Modular structural building system

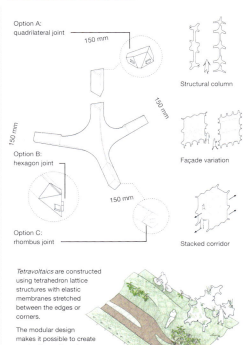

Tetravoltaics are constructed using tetrahedron lattice structures with elastic membranes stretched between the edges or corners.

The modular design makes it possible to create applications with various configurations and scales ranging from benches to greenhouse structures.

Flower Power: Forever in Bloom

DESIGNERS: Jinmo Jung, Michael Goode, Kayesten Jade Caluag, Daryl Gonzales, Maciej Dwojak (WE Design)

ENERGY TECHNOLOGY: monocrystalline solar photovoltaic, triboelectric fabric

ANNUAL PRODUCTION: 1,000 MWh

OTHER SOCIAL CO-BENEFITS: personal electronic device charging, public Wi-Fi

Flower Power celebrates the 2023 German Federal Horticulture Show with an homage to the national flower of Germany, the cornflower, with its striking blue hue. Two types of energy sculptures engage the public with solar power and kinetic energy harvesting technologies.

The stems of each flower contain charging points for devices such as mobile phones and laptops. The petals of the first type of flower incorporate triboelectric nanogenerator fabric that converts the movement of the material in the wind into electrical power. Four thousand of this type of flower sculpture are distributed throughout the park with their focus along the wind channels of the Climate Corridor. Triboelectric fiber has ultra-thin zinc oxide coated wires woven in one direction and gold wires aligned in another direction. When the fabric is stretched or twisted, the two wires rub against each other and create static electricity due to the different nature of their conductivity, in the same way as a rubber balloon will generate static shocks when rubbed against human hair.

The second type of flower-inspired energy sculpture integrates photovoltaic cells in a range of blue shades into the petal of the flower. One hundred and fifty of these flowers are arranged throughout the park to take advantage of sunlight and complement energy production on days without wind.

Bioluminescent tubes line the petals to produce an ambient blue light at night, creating a magical setting amongst the meadow of sculptural cornflowers.

The German national flower, the cornflower, is the same beautiful blue that is commonly associated with renewable energy.

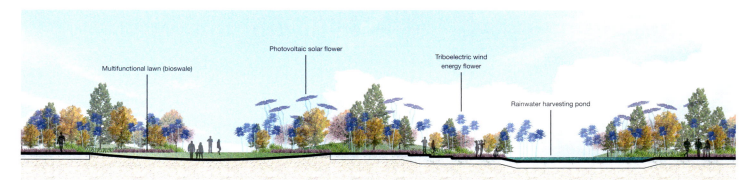

Part of the energy accumulated in the flower's batteries is used to power the LED lights providing a glowing spectacle at night.

Planktonic Synergy

DESIGNER: Chen-Hsiang Chao

ENERGY TECHNOLOGY: organic photovoltaic (OPV) solar, compressed air energy storage (CAES)

ANNUAL PRODUCTION: 3,450 MWh

OTHER SOCIAL CO-BENEFITS: fresh and cool air to combat urban heat, shaded gathering spaces

Planktonic Synergy is a series of dynamic climatic devices located throughout the landscape that respond to changing weather conditions. The devices store and release fresh air dynamically to create a beneficial microclimate and support Spinelli Park's role as a Climate Corridor for the city.

The floating structures are made from ETFE with integrated organic photovoltaic solar film, inflated with helium, and anchored by wire cables attached to the ground. Beneath the structure, a wind-condensing turbine pulls in air when renewable electricity is plentiful on the grid, compressing and storing it in underground tanks, and releasing it when renewable energy is scarce. This energy storage component allows for more intermittent renewable energy resources to be added to the grid. The floating structure stays low when the device is inhaling air and rises toward the sky when the compressed air is released.

The primary benefit of the release of compressed air is to generate electricity, some of which is used to light the LED disks attached to the wire cables, creating a futuristic and poetic spatial experience for visitors. The cold air released from underground also helps to cool the environment, assisting the Climate Corridor in its work to reduce the heat island effects in the city.

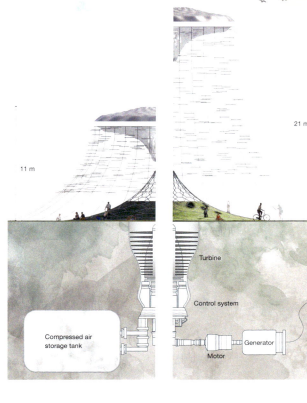

The artwork changes throughout the day. In the morning the floating structures stay low while they gather the sun's energy and store it underground in compressed air storage tanks.

In the evening the air is released, generating electricity for the grid during peak demand while cooling the air that flows into the center of the city.

The Energy+Art Garden

DESIGNERS: Nina Colosi, Raphaele Shirley, Claude Boullevraye de Passillé, Bernardo Zavattini

ENERGY TECHNOLOGY: organic Rankine cycle low-temperature geothermal (Climeon or similar), concentrated solar power (CSP) thermal, thin-film solar photovoltaic (SoloPower Systems Inc. or similar), kinetic energy harvesting (Pavegen or similar)

ANNUAL PRODUCTION: 10,000 MWh

OTHER SOCIAL CO-BENEFITS: hydroponic urban farming, public space for gathering, personal electronic device charging

The Energy+Art Garden (TEAG) immerses visitors in a futurist's world of dramatic energy production, reactive sculpture and lighting, lush plantings, and pathways connecting gathering points for public engagement within Spinelli Park. During the day, night, and throughout all seasons, the beauty and multisensory experience of *TEAG* sparks the imaginations of visitors and instills in them a desire for a world powered by clean energy.

TEAG starts from the design forms that have been central to the social systems of civilizations throughout history and augments them with twenty-first-century technologies that unlock the energies of the earth and sun. These forms — mound, ziggurat, pyramid, arena, and circle — are used for agriculture, community, ceremony, cosmology, cultural and spiritual meaning, and aligning with the symbiosis of humans and the cycles of nature.

TEAG is a self-sustaining oasis that provides energy to the grid using geothermal, solar, and kinetic energy technologies. Energy production supports *TEAG*'s integrated systems, including its maintenance, community programming, and the composting of organic waste. The compost supports the hanging gardens that grow vegetables, such as butternut squash and spinach.

A low-temperature geothermal system is installed under the Energy Mound sculpture. The ground loop taps into the 55-degree Celsius hot water one kilometer below the city, which is located in the Upper Rhine Rift — one of Germany's three regions with geothermal activity. Some of the heat is used directly for space heating, and the balance is converted into electricity with an organic Rankine cycle generator. Other artworks, such as the Concentrator, heat a transfer fluid to the same temperature using solar energy. The public project highlights Germany's plan to supply half of its heating sector with shallow and deep geothermal by 2050.

Thin-film photovoltaic is integrated into the sky-facing elements of the artworks, especially the Solar Pavilion and Data Lightways. Kinetic energy pavers harvest the footfall traffic of park-goers to support lighting, irrigation, heating, maintenance, agriculture, charging stations, exercise, and programs for entertainment and play.

The Solar Pavilion

The Energy Sphere is an ETFE and PTFE inflatable form anchored within a water basin with concrete and aircraft cable ties.

A motorized tracking system orients the opening toward the sun to harvest electricity and hot water using photovoltaic modules and a thermodynamic generator.

Hanging Garden incorporates concentric circles for hydroponic gardening, seed collection, programs, and performances. Stored solar energy illuminates its pattern at night creating a light sculpture.

Data Lightways incorporates photovoltaic panels and kinetic floor tiles onto a 3D printed structure. The archways display the total amount of energy generated by *TEAG*.

MOUND

DESIGNERS: Iman Khalili, Puya Khalili, Aziz Khalili
ENERGY TECHNOLOGY: solar photovoltaic
ANNUAL PRODUCTION: 20,000 MWh
OTHER SOCIAL CO-BENEFITS: urban agriculture, water harvesting and purification

There are few major cities in the world whose civic symbol celebrates water like the Mannheim Wasserturm does. The story of Mannheim and its battle for clean and pure water spans centuries — a community intent on surviving in a land with little access to clean ground water has taught us a lesson on what it means to fight for clean water with ingenuity and innovation, and finally emerge victorious, having a water tower in the center of town to show for it.

In the presence of this town's relentless spirit of innovation and its appreciation of technology, MOUND is a new public space that — just like its predecessor, the Wasserturm — creates a space for people to enjoy and appreciate the life-giving presence of water and introduce the public to new technologies.

MOUND is a self-sustaining structure. It serves as an elevated landmark, in an otherwise flat metropolitan area, for people to gather and enjoy the presence of water and nature in a very distinct and transcendental space.

All the electrical energy needed to operate the installation is captured through integrated photovoltaic modules and stored in batteries within the body of MOUND. Groundwater and water retained year-round from precipitation is purified by the artwork through sand filtration, reverse osmosis, and ozonation. This pure water in turn flows through the space, giving life to a lush garden spiraling around the outer surface of the mound.

This is the story of water and the beauty it can create when technological innovation, architectural design, and nature come together. It is a learning playground within which to witness the water cycle from precipitation to evaporation.

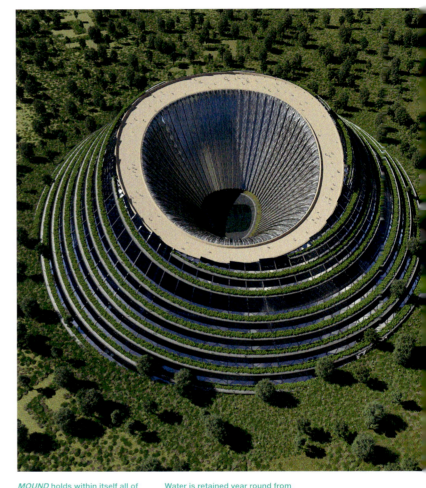

The installation provides a space for public engagement through public gardens. The gardens are laid out across MOUND, between sections dedicated to solar panels. The space underneath MOUND stores a water treatment unit, a small power plant, a pump house, and groundwater submersible pumps, as well as rainwater collection basins.

MOUND holds within itself all of the technological features that allow it to be a self-sufficient unit. All of the electrical energy needed to operate the structure is captured through photovoltaic panels, and stored in batteries within the body of the artwork.

Water is retained year round from precipitation and groundwater and purified within the structure. This clean water flows through the artwork, giving life to the lush garden spiraling around the outer surface, then cycles back through the central pond.

Flower Farm

DESIGNER: Andreea Ștefan
ENERGY TECHNOLOGY: organic photovoltaic (OPV) solar
ANNUAL PRODUCTION: 1.3 MWh per large flower sculpture
OTHER SOCIAL CO-BENEFITS: shaded space for resting and growing plants

We find ourselves in a transition between a human culture that separates the artificial world from the natural world and a future that promises a greater symbiosis between nature and technology. As a creative product of this transition, *Flower Farm* blends technological and natural systems to bring this new age of symbiosis into greater public consciousness.

Flower Farm absorbs sunlight and collects rainwater, stimulating natural growth and providing a beautiful shading device in the landscape. The petals of the flower are composed of a smart organic photovoltaic material that is fabricated in a variety of colors. Its wavy shape is not only beautiful to behold, but it provides a larger surface area for solar power generation. The semitransparent organic photovoltaic (OPV) material of the flower petals converts certain spectra of sunlight into electricity while allowing the light range most useful for photosynthesis to pass through to the ground plane.

Along the stem of the flower, planter boxes host flowers, aromatic plants, vegetables, and fruits. Within the stem flows energy for the city grid and water for irrigation. The base of the flower doubles as a park bench and planter, while providing space for water and energy storage inside.

The petals of *Flower Farm* collect rainwater and sunlight.

The flower stem provides space for water and energy flow.

The leaves of the flower are small planters that are irrigated from the collected rainwater. Each component is designed to slot together with any other component for an expanding kit of parts.

Instead of roots, the flower has a base that provides storage for energy and water, additional planting areas, and benches.

Exploded diagram of *Flower Farm* components

Flower Farm can be installed at the scale of a private kleingarten. The electricity it generates at this scale is sufficient to provide lighting and to power a small garden house.

The Solar Poplars

DESIGNERS: Miroslaw Struzik, Jakub Skowron, Hafis Hermann Issa, Olivier Portier

ENERGY TECHNOLOGY: organic photovoltaic (OPV) solar (similar to ASCA®)

ANNUAL PRODUCTION: 5 MWh per year per set of ten large leaves

OTHER SOCIAL CO-BENEFITS: personal device charging, food production

The Solar Poplars reimagines the abstract natural form of the poplar leaf with photovoltaics in place of photosynthesis. The leaf modules are introduced into the park as artworks, creating a visual symbol of sustainable development while generating useful energy for the public.

The modules come in three sizes and can be easily installed to beautify and electrify any number of outdoor spaces. When installed next to garden rows, *The Solar Poplars* can provide just the right amount of shade to reduce irrigation requirements. The active photovoltaic element is a lamination of two layers of polycarbonate, integrating semi-translucent organic PV modules made by ASCA® and fabricated in Germany.

Thanks to a laser structuring method, the modules can take on any shape and size while maintaining a relatively low cost of production. Organic photovoltaic technology has an even lower embodied CO_2 content than conventional solar panels and an energy payback period of between three and six months — less than half that of monocrystalline silicon modules.

At night *The Solar Poplars* create a stunning environment with integrated LED lighting powered by a small percentage of the energy generated during the day, most of which is sent to the grid to help power the lives of Mannheim's citizens.

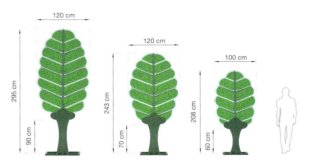

The Solar Poplars take the form of a simplified, symbolic tree and are designed in three sizes.

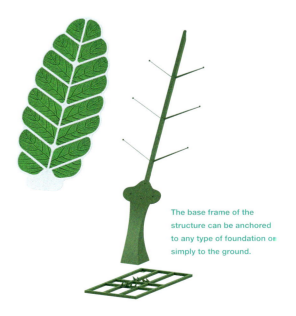

The base frame of the structure can be anchored to any type of foundation or simply to the ground.

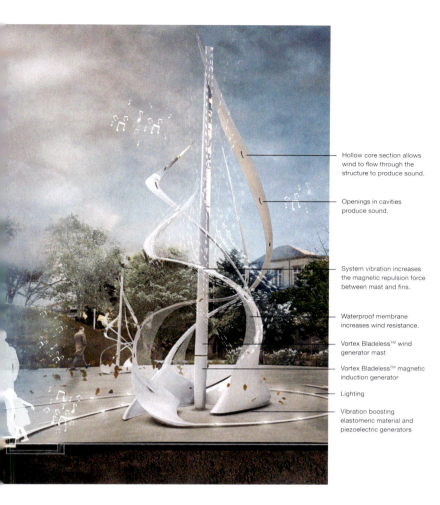

Some of the energy generated is used to power an experimental research site that explores the potential benefits of magnetohydrodynamics, which uses vibration energy to lower the surface tension of water, creating greater solubility and penetration, which may stimulate root systems.

Vibranergy: Energy Turned Into Vibrancy

DESIGNERS: Daniela Lucia Arguello Munive, Julieth Alejandra Garcia Molano, Diego Alexis Avella Castro, Ricardo Andres Ibanez Gutierrez, Juan Sebastian Vaca Porras, Angelica Maria Pineda Sierra, Maria Paula Correa Munoz, Laura Fernanda Pedraza Tamayo

ENERGY TECHNOLOGY: bladeless wind power (similar to Vortex Bladeless™), vibration-induced electromagnetic induction, piezoelectric generators

ANNUAL PRODUCTION: 400 MWh

OTHER SOCIAL CO-BENEFITS: electronic device charging, public spaces for gathering

Wind jostling the branches of a tree. The chance of a falling leaf. A crackling fire on a moonless summer night. These beautiful and mesmerizing movements have influenced music and philosophy for centuries. *Vibranergy* is an energy-generating artwork that celebrates mesmerizing moments and the wonder of life, while engaging citizens within an immersive orchestral experience.

Mannheim has played an important role in the history of music. An entire orchestral technique is named the Mannheim School, and the city influenced the work of Wolfgang Amadeus Mozart. *Vibranergy* revives the musical roots of Mannheim to create a set of hot spots that foster community gatherings and help provide energy and food security.

The centerpiece of each sculptural gathering place is a "bonfire" of vibrating metal that conceals applications of the latest advancements in renewable energy technology, including piezoelectric generators and bladeless wind power—vibration-induced electromagnetic induction. In the very center, a Vortex Bladeless™ wind turbine generates energy as it vibrates in the wind. The center is surrounded by spiraling arms, like circling flames, that at some angles call to mind a treble clef symbol. At key locations in the arms, magnets generate additional energy from periodic waves of movement as the arms nearly touch then pull away. Piezoelectric pads in the foundation of the arms generate additional electricity through the pressure applied by the motion.

Inspired by the wind and string instruments played by musicians of the Mannheim School since the late eighteenth century, the flame-like arms of the sculpture include resonance chambers and air channels that sing softly with the flow of the surrounding wind. The vibration of the arms generates a rhythm for the notes. The effect is mesmerizing and provides a beautiful setting for gatherings and celebrations.

Bloom: Purpose of Nature

DESIGNERS: Pranshu Agrawal, Denise Marie Angel De Leon Galano, James Ndiritu Gachari

ENERGY TECHNOLOGY: monocrystalline solar photovoltaic

ANNUAL PRODUCTION: 5,000 MWh

OTHER SOCIAL CO-BENEFITS: shaded spaces for gathering, food production in solar greenhouses

Our society and economy, our very existence, is made possible by nature and yet we are too often unaware of our connection to the earth — that it is the foundation of our wellbeing. *Bloom* depicts the purpose of nature and reminds us of our oneness with it. Large flower-like and bud-like structures incorporate solar photovoltaic technology and connect local communities with a healthy environment.

Flower-like structures offer views of Mannheim day and night and offer protection to elm, maple, and birch trees that live in symbiosis with the artwork, their mature growth size fitting perfectly within the canopy of the flower's petals. As the sun rises, the flower-like petals open to provide shade and energy. In the evening as the sun sets, the petals close and become site lights and wayfinding beacons.

Steel mesh structures of support double as water harvesting mechanisms, drawing moisture from morning condensation, and channeling it to collection cisterns for irrigation use.

Bud-like structures take the form of domes embedded on the ground. These structures serve as meeting spaces and greenhouses that grow through all seasons warmed by the natural sunlight that flows through solar panel glazing.

Curious park visitors can look out over the entire site from the viewing platforms and see the paths connecting the flower-like artworks.

Flower-like structures open as the sun rises using a sun tracker embedded in the solar panels that identifies the sun's position throughout the day.

Solar panels are placed on the petals of the flower-like structure absorbing natural sunlight and creating electricity used throughout the site.

Flower Garden

DESIGNER: Brent Haynes
ENERGY TECHNOLOGY: horizontal axis wind turbine
ANNUAL PRODUCTION: 20 MWh
OTHER SOCIAL CO-BENEFITS: creative placemaking, lighted pathways

Wind turbines in the near distance look curiously like sculptural adaptations of the flowers that sway with gentle rhythm on the pleasantly warm evening breeze beneath a deep blue sky. A couple takes their afternoon stroll along the old railway tracks of Spinelli Park. As the sun begins to set, the turbine-powered lights softly illuminate their path guiding them home.

The proportions of common wind farms today do not consider the human scale. *Flower Garden* merges the spatial scale of the wind turbine with the scale of park-goers by converting wind turbine infrastructure into sculptural elements that enhance public space and beautify Spinelli Park.

Native flowers of Mannheim are the source of inspiration. The design of the flower-inspired wind turbines changes based on their scale. Larger turbines are more sculptural and operate at the city scale. Medium size turbines are the scale of allotment gardens and incorporate elements of floral design motifs. The smaller turbines at individual scale are the most flower-like, designed to limit visual interruption by blending into the surroundings.

Medium scale and small scale versions of the whimsical *Flower Garden* wind turbines support life in kleingärten of Mannheim.

Flower Garden brings the wind turbine back into the city at a human scale, connecting us to nature and to our energy production for a brighter future.

Walking in the Fields of Gold

DESIGNER: Jason Kim

ENERGY TECHNOLOGY: dye-sensitized solar cell (DSSC), kinetic energy pavers

ANNUAL PRODUCTION: 1,300 MWh

OTHER SOCIAL CO-BENEFITS: shaded gathering space, urban farming, water harvesting

Solar power technology has been around for hundreds of years, yet it is seldom celebrated as a design element.

Walking in the Fields of Gold is an art installation that integrates solar, wind, and kinetic-energy harvesting in Mannheim's Spinelli Park. Modular, 5-meter cube canopies define follies in the landscape, supporting an artwork that meanders overhead made from a golden-tinted dye-sensitized solar cell (DSSC) woven fabric. As this energy fabric waves in the breezes flowing across the Climate Corridor, it generates motion that is harnessed by piezoelectric actuators. On the ground level, kinetic energy pavers turn the play and footsteps of park-goers into even more electricity.

The site is both a public solar park and an agricultural landscape defined by 15-meter-wide agricultural strips of land, growing fresh food over a portion of the public park and leaving the rest to open space and native hare and lizard habitat. The structures harvest two-million liters of stormwater per year that are used to irrigate the crops and gardens of Spinelli Park.

Each module consists of wooden structural members, DSSC fabric, piezoelectric pavers, and/or water collection modules. The three-dimensional grid layout allows the system to be expanded horizontally and vertically to meet the power needs of its adjacent community or to take advantage of its natural environment.

The DSSC substrate uses a kinetic textile consisting of conductive multi-walled carbon nanotubes with polyethylene terephthalate wires giving it weather protection and structural resilience. The battery is integrated into the fabric and responds automatically to changing site demand conditions.

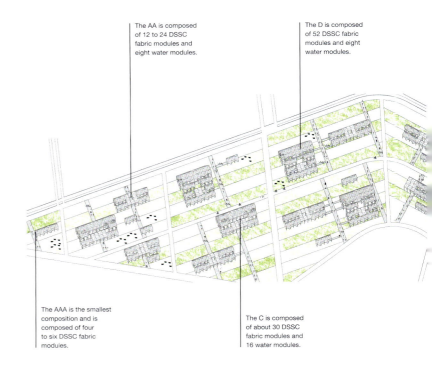

The AA is composed of 12 to 24 DSSC fabric modules and eight water modules.

The D is composed of 52 DSSC fabric modules and eight water modules.

The AAA is the smallest composition and is composed of four to six DSSC fabric modules.

The C is composed of about 30 DSSC fabric modules and 16 water modules.

Walking in the Fields of Gold is composed of various modular arrangements that correlate to the universal battery sizes, ranging from AAA through D.

DSSC fabric modules

DSSC fabric modules comprise 29 square meters of dye-sensitized solar cell fabric coated in acrylic for protection.

Water modules

Water modules are stainless steel water collecting devices with a reservoir base.

Piezoelectric pavers

Piezoelectric pavers collect kinetic energy from pedestrian's footsteps.

Walking in the Fields of Gold is a series of modular follies.

Windwald

DESIGNERS: Andrew Park, Gun Hee Jeong, Sung Uk Choi, Seung Hoon Lee, Jong Chan Jeon, Eun Mee Jeong, Song Hyeok Oh

ENERGY TECHNOLOGY: triboelectric nanogenerator (TENG)

ANNUAL PRODUCTION: 2,000 MWh

OTHER SOCIAL CO-BENEFITS: shaded gathering spaces

***Windwald* is a glimpse** into the wonder of life in a sustainable city. This artful energy landscape produces clean electricity from the wind in collaboration with the activities of the people who visit Spinelli Park.

The installation is informed by the planned Climate Corridor, a network of open spaces that will bring fresh air from the nearby Vogelstangsee Park and the forested areas to the northeast, into Spinelli Park and the City of Mannheim.

The structure of each tree-like form is composed of recycled plywood and is designed to support the generator module pendants. The structure comes in two sizes, which are situated with regard to location and program. Spherical triboelectric generator modules hang on wires suspended from the plywood structure in rows of four or five. Each module pendant is covered with insulating material that protects electric wires, an LED diode, an aluminum conductor plate, and the triboelectric generator.

Triboelectric nanogenerators (TENG) generate electricity by harnessing kinetic energy from nature. As two materials with very different properties are placed in frictional contact (like a rubber balloon on human hair), they generate static electricity. A cathode and anode are affixed to the material and harness this electrical energy into a current. Though the amount of energy from the single module is minimal, the sum of several modules connected in series produces a significant amount of electricity.

As the *Windwald* modules are suspended in the path of the continuous flow of air across Spinelli Park, the wind creates friction in the TENG modules and the landscape becomes a large and magical renewable energy generator. As park visitors pass by and touch the modules out of curiosity, they add to the amount of electricity produced.

The arrangement of the tree-like forms around the site creates plazas for gathering and private spaces for meditation. At night the generator modules glow white, providing a soft illumination and a pleasant atmosphere while creating a feeling of being surrounded by falling stars.

Windwald is a new form of garden — an energy garden!

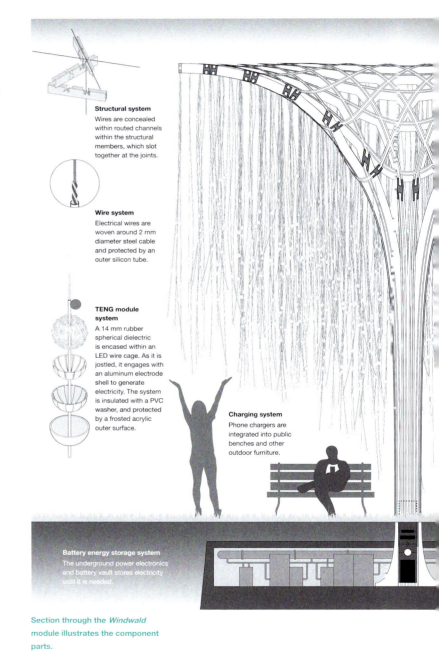

Section through the *Windwald* module illustrates the component parts.

LED lighting that is synchronized with real-time power generation creates a dynamic energyscape when the wind blows and gives park-goers a visceral awareness of how much energy is being harnessed at any one time.

A Celebration of Light, Water, and Mirror

DESIGNERS: Shahed M. Yengiabad, Elaheh M. Yengiabad, Alemeh M. Yengiabad
ENERGY TECHNOLOGY: perovskite solar photovoltaic
ANNUAL PRODUCTION: 300 MWh
OTHER SOCIAL CO-BENEFITS: bioluminescent lighting, playful public engagement

Light has a special place in human life. Our ancestors considered light sacred and its source, the sun, life-giving. The brightness of the days began with the sunrise and ended with the sunset. For this reason, our ancestors often spoke of a battle between light and darkness, or between good and evil. They considered light as hope, life, and happiness, and darkness as the end, despair, and sorrow. At the beginning of each day, light wins over darkness and awakens hope.

When the mirror was invented, it came to be seen within this metaphysical context. The joy and warmth of life was multiplied by the mirror's reflections. The Mesopotamians and Egyptians considered the mirror to be one of the components of the human soul because, like water, it was a symbol of purity and honesty, a reflection of the truth. The mirror is therefore a reminder of endless hope, a hope that began from a source far from the reach of humans— the sun.

A Celebration of Light, Water, and Mirror uses the confluence of light, water, and mirror as circular gates conceptually connected to another dimension. The form of circles illustrates the idea of time and movement without beginning or end. A cross section of each ring is triangular, with its three sides symbolizing the sun, the moon, and the stars or light, mirror, and water.

Two of the three sides of the rings are covered with phosphorescent paint that absorbs light during the day and reflects it at night to illuminate the park. The outside face of each ring is clad with perovskite photovoltaic material, which converts absorbed light into electricity for use on site. With hundreds of rings spanning radially from the center of the park and over 1,000 square meters of surface area, *A Celebration of Light, Water, and Mirror* will contribute significantly to the energy needs of the city.

There are a total of six different size rings that are spread out at various angles around a central point on the site. Two of the three sides of the rings are covered with phosphorescent paint that absorbs light during the day and reflects it at night. The outer side of each ring contains a solar panel made of perovskite, which converts absorbed light into electricity.

The Sun Flower installed at the kleingarten scale can provide 100% of the energy demand of the garden.

The Sun Flower installed in a civic park helps to power public places.

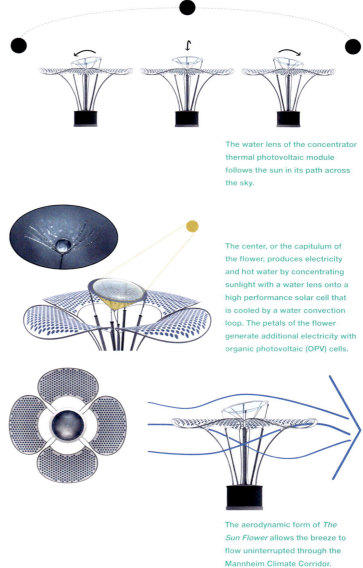

The water lens of the concentrator thermal photovoltaic module follows the sun in its path across the sky.

The center, or the capitulum of the flower, produces electricity and hot water by concentrating sunlight with a water lens onto a high performance solar cell that is cooled by a water convection loop. The petals of the flower generate additional electricity with organic photovoltaic (OPV) cells.

The aerodynamic form of *The Sun Flower* allows the breeze to flow uninterrupted through the Mannheim Climate Corridor.

The Sun Flower

DESIGNERS: Sam Arab Oveissi, Pedram Salimi, Shadi Razani, Golnoush Parsi, Jalal Arab Oveissi
ENERGY TECHNOLOGY: concentrator thermal photovoltaic, organic photovoltaic (OPV)
ANNUAL PRODUCTION: 4 MWh per module
OTHER SOCIAL CO-BENEFITS: shaded gathering space, public device charging

The more the members of a society are connected, the more they learn from each other and flourish. *The Sun Flower* is a gathering place for people that provides shade and clean energy, encouraging people to come together and engage.

The design is modular and scalable. It can be used as a single structure in a private area or multiple structures can serve a public commons. The materials are low cost, organic, and low embodied energy.

Each module is like a four-petaled flower. In the center is a water-filled lens that tracks the sun's position in the sky using hydraulic piston supports. The water lens concentrates sunlight onto a high-performance multi-junction solar cell that is cooled using a water heat sink. The hot water can be used locally to heat greenhouses, warm benches, or make additional electricity. Covering the petals of the flower are organic photovoltaic (OPV) solar cells arranged in a hexagonal pattern inspired by nature.

The Sun Flower spread across Spinelli Park provides a recognizable symbol of sustainability and serves the needs of park-goers for shade and connectivity.

Eco-Art Pollinators

DESIGNERS: Andrew King, Gaston Fernandez, Vicky Jia Bao Wang, Laura Di Fiore, Jasper Silver-King, Jeffrey Ma
ENERGY TECHNOLOGY: thin-film solar photovoltaic balloons
ANNUAL PRODUCTION: 2,000 MWh
OTHER SOCIAL CO-BENEFITS: biodiversity, pollinator habitat and research

Eco-Art Pollinators is a series of landscape art interventions throughout Spinelli Park that shift the public's relationship to ecological issues. By prioritizing habitats and pollinating corridors, the artwork brings varied and biodiverse life back to the site and reminds park-goers of their individual agency in the cultural transition toward greater stewardship of nature.

The site is designed through multiple layers. Maintaining the ground as a living ecosystem, solar balloons extend the park into the sky and above the cloud line. The balloons collect energy that feeds back into the surrounding neighborhood while delighting visitors with their playful and instantly recognizable form. The dark, thin-film solar photovoltaic exterior of each balloon generates electricity and also heat, which is passed directly into the balloon interior to maintain buoyancy, keeping the solar technology cool on the outside and operating at peak efficiency. A lightweight and low-cost solution, the solar balloons are eventually deployed around the city, in public spaces and private gardens, quickly becoming an identifiable symbol of Mannheim's commitment to an equitable energy transition.

In the shadow of the solar balloons, the ground-based landscape interventions address the rapidly declining pollinator ecosystem. Hyperhabitats are established in and around a series of four types of tower installations made from recycled wood, mycelium, and gabions. Diverse systems of plants, fungi, and invertebrates act as productive nodes for expanding pollinator networks, interconnected by pathways for walking, cycling, and running — places for physical activity, rest, observation, and circulation.

Pollinator corridors

The site is a place for environmental research, experimentation, learning, and innovation. In addition to offering a wide variety of uses and activities, *Eco-Art Pollinators* exists as a habitat and pollination corridor, increasing ecological connectivity by preserving four endangered species in Mannheim: the long-eared bat, crested lark, wall lizard, and mason bee.

The planting strategy offers a display of visual delight with nectar-rich wildflowers in blue and violet — colors that are attractive to the mason bee, butterflies, flies, and other insects. New trees provide additional habitat and sequester carbon from the air.

Organic tower forms serve as hyperhabitats to support local pollinator species, connecting Spinelli Park visitors to the complexity of the local ecosystem and the resources it generates.

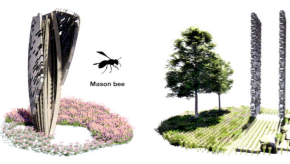

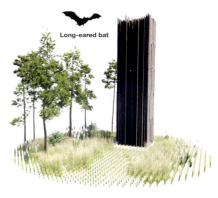

Mason bee · Wall lizard · Crested lark · Long-eared bat

Hyperhabitats for local endangered species

Ecological education
Visitors learn about tree biomass, biodiversity, carbon sequestration, local cooling effects, and reduced heat loads.

Flora and fauna community
The artwork creates a nurturing environment, promotes good soil drainage, and reduces environmental pollutants.

223

BIOGRAPHIES, GLOSSARY, INDEX, AND ACKNOWLEDGMENTS

BIOGRAPHIES

ROBERT FERRY

Robert Ferry is the founding co-director of the Land Art Generator Initiative and Studied Impact Design. Before co-founding the Land Art Generator Initiative in 2008, he collaborated with project management and design teams delivering sustainable and LEED-certified projects ranging from custom single-family residential to $500 million CAPEX mixed-use and corporate campuses. He spent four years as a consultant on large commercial projects in Abu Dhabi, where his focus shifted to ways in which buildings can move beyond net-zero and contribute to the regenerative infrastructure of the surrounding city. His concept designs pushing the envelope of building-integrated renewable energy technology have been published widely. Through the Land Art Generator Initiative, he supports the critical role of architecture and urban design as part of a comprehensive solution to climate change. Robert is a graduate of Carnegie Mellon University and a LEED-accredited licensed architect.

As co-director of LAGI he has received multiple National Endowment for the Arts grants and has been awarded the J.M.K. Innovation Prize, a program of the J.M. Kaplan Fund.His publications include *Land Art of the 21st Century*, *Regenerative Infrastructures*, *The Time Is Now: Public Art of the Sustainable City*, *New Energies*, *Powering Places*, *Energy Overlays*, *Return to the Source*, and *A Field Guide to Renewable Energy*.

ELIZABETH MONOIAN

Elizabeth Monoian is the founding co-director of the Land Art Generator Initiative (LAGI). In this role she is developing global partnerships between private and public entities around interdisciplinary projects that address issues of climate and sustainability through the lens of creativity. She works closely with cities, universities, corporations, arts organizations, and community groups to design customized approaches to renewable energy installations.

She has published, exhibited, and presented globally on the aesthetics of renewable energy and the role of art in providing solutions to the climate crises. Under her leadership, LAGI has received multiple National Endowment for the Arts grants and has been awarded the J.M.K. Innovation Prize, a program of the J.M. Kaplan Fund. She holds an MFA from Carnegie Mellon University.

Her publications include *Land Art of the 21st Century*, *Regenerative Infrastructures*, *The Time Is Now: Public Art of the Sustainable City*, *New Energies*, *Powering Places*, *Energy Overlays*, *Return to the Source*, and *A Field Guide to Renewable Energy*.

TINA NAILOR

Tina Nailor holds a Bachelor of Arts in Urban Studies from the University of Washington, Tacoma. Her passion is in inclusive urban design with community and sustainability at its center. Tina grew up in Viernheim, Germany surrounded by kleingärten and bicycle paths. These key memories are embedded in her advocacy for sustainable green spaces that bring together individual cultures, creating communities and memories. Her diverse background and education give her a unique insight into the global connection of cities and their possibilities for a greener and diverse future.

BIOGRAPHIES (continued)

ANN ROSENTHAL

As an artist, educator, and writer, Ann has interrogated the intersections of nature and culture through a range of environmental issues for more than four decades. Over the last few years, Ann has returned to her creative roots in painting and printmaking, celebrating her love of color, gesture, and form in nature and art. She is particularly drawn to places where water and land meet — fragile ecosystems that we endanger through ignorance, desire, and greed. Ann's recent creative and professional accomplishments include: Artist in Residence, HJ Andrews Experimental Forest, Oregon (2018); Co-Curator for "Crafting Conversations: A Call and Response to Our Changing Climate," Contemporary Craft BNY Mellon Gallery (2019); awarded "Woman of Environmental Art" from PennFuture (2020); one of four editors for *Ecoart in Action: Activities, Case Studies, and Provocations for Classrooms and Communities* (New Village Press, 2022); selected to design and execute two asphalt art murals with collaborator JoAnn Moran for Friendship Park in Pittsburgh, PA (2022–2023). Ann received her MFA from Carnegie Mellon University in 1999.

PAUL SCHIFINO

Paul received his degree in graphic design from the Art Institute of Pittsburgh in 1979. His work has been published in design publications including *Communication Arts (CA)*, *Graphis*, *Print*, *How*, and *ReadyMade* magazine. His art has been included in shows at The Andy Warhol Museum (*AMP*), the Mattress Factory (*Gestures #4* and *#14*), TRAF Gallery (*By Design*), TRAF Gallery (*Best of Pittsburgh Show*), and most recently *The John Show*. His work is also included in the permanent archive of the Mattress Factory.

He has served as president of the Pittsburgh chapter of the American Institute of Graphic Arts (AIGA), and is a former Advisory Board member of the American Shorts Reading Series, and the Art Institute of Pittsburgh. Paul currently serves on the Board of the Land Art Generator Initiative

MICHAEL SCHNELLBACH

Michael Schnellbach was born in Heidelberg in 1964. He studied administrative sciences and worked from 1989 to 2017 for the City of Mannheim. After holding various positions within the city administration, including Head of the Misdemeanor Department and clerk in facilities management, he became the commercial manager of the "m:con-mannheim:congress GmbH" in 2008. From 2011 to 2017, Michael Schnellbach was Head of the Department of Citizens' Services of the City of Mannheim. During this time, he had already been the part-time Managing Director of the "Bundesgartenschau Mannheim 2023 gGmbH" since 2014; since 2017, he has performed this task full-time. Michael Schnellbach is married and has two daughters.

ALESSANDRA SCOGNAMIGLIO

A licensed architect, Alessandra Scognamiglio did a Master's Degree in Architecture at the University of Naples before completing a PhD in Technologies for Architecture and the Environment at the University of Campania. Since 2000, she has been a researcher in ENEA's Energy Technologies and Renewable Sources Department, where she works on the use of photovoltaics in buildings and the landscape.

Scognamiglio was recently appointed president of the Italian Association for Sustainable Agrivoltaics, and she is also coordinator of ENEA's new Sustainable Agrivoltaics Taskforce, which supports the establishment of a national sustainable agrivoltaics network with members from institutions, professional associations, academia, and the business world.

Scognamiglio's own research work focuses on the adoption of trans-disciplinary perspectives which become innovative cognitive frameworks capable of creating new design visions for photovoltaics.

The author of over 100 published articles and the holder of several patents, Scognamiglio has been an organizer for the Photovoltaics and Integration into Buildings and the Landscape topic for the European Photovoltaics Conference and in 2022 she was the general chair of the 8th World Conference on Photovoltaic Energy Conversion. She is also the founder and president of the annual "Photovoltaics | Forms | Landscapes" event.

SVEN STREMKE

Sven Stremke is Associate Professor for Landscape Architecture at Wageningen University in The Netherlands, Principal Investigator at the Amsterdam Institute for Advanced Metropolitan Solutions, and founding director of the NRGlab, a research laboratory on energy transition. Sven practiced as a landscape architect in Germany, the United States, Spain, and the Netherlands before joining academia. His research and teaching focus on the relations between renewable energy and the living environment.

Sven has co-authored more than 25 scientific papers and many book chapters on planning and design for energy transition. Together with Dirk Oudes and Paolo Picchi, he published the book *The Power of Landscape: Novel Narratives to Engage with the Energy Transition* in 2022 (nai010, Rotterdam). In 2018, Sven participated in the negotiations of the Dutch National Climate Agreement as an expert for landscapes-related questions. Sven is a member of the scientific advisory committees for the German Academy for Territorial Development in the Leibnitz Association (ARL) and the Dutch National Consortium Sun & Landscape (NCZiL). Sven is scientific director of the WUR Solar Research Programme, initiator of the Wageningen Energy Alliance, and board member of the Dutch Archiprix foundation.

GLOSSARY

ABSORPTION
A process by which ions, molecules, or atoms are taken up into the volume of a material.

ABSORPTION CHILLER
A refrigeration system that uses heat energy (such as that from the sun) to drive the cooling process. The system is a closed loop containing a solution of a low-boiling point refrigerant (e.g. ammonia or lithium bromide) and an absorbant (e.g. a salt solution). At various stages the refrigerant is either evaporated from, or absorbed into the water. The process was invented by the French scientist Ferdinand Carré in 1858 using sulfuric acid. One variation is referred to as the Einstein refrigerator, patented by Albert Einstein and his former student Leó Szilárd. Adsorption (with a "d") refrigeration systems are similar, except that the refrigerant is not absorbed into a liquid, but rather adsorbs onto the surface of a solid, such as a silicone gel.

ADSORPTION
A process by which ions, molecules, or atoms adhere to the outer surface of a material.

AEROPONICS
A soil-less plant growing process using water or mist to provide nutrients (type of hydroponics). This method significantly reduces water, fertilizer, and pesticide compared to open field agriculture while maximizing the crop yields.

AGRIVOLTAIC
Sharing land use for simultaneous solar energy production and food production. In sunny and arid climates, the use of solar panels to partially shade crops can increase yields.

ALGAE BIOFUEL
Algae can be grown and harvested (algaculture) as a feed stock for the production of alternatives to fossil fuels. Naturally occurring oils within algae (lipids) can be used directly (similar to straight vegetable oil), or they can be refined to burn more cleanly. Different production methods can result in biodiesel, biobutanol, biogasoline, methane, ethanol, or even jet fuel. The uptake of CO_2 by the algae during cultivation offsets the CO_2 that is emitted during the combustion of the algae-generated fuel.

ALGAE PHOTOBIOREACTOR
A bioreactor that uses sunlight to cultivate algae that require sun and CO_2 for the processing of nutrients. The resulting algae biomass can be used to create a variety of biofuels and other products.

ANAEROBIC DIGESTER (BIODIGESTER)
A system that allows organic matter (biomass) to decompose through natural biotic processes within an oxygen-poor (anaerobic) environment to produce biogas. The gas byproduct of anaerobic biodigestion is mostly methane and is similar in composition to conventional natural gas. It can be used for many different purposes including cooking, heating, lighting, transportation, and electricity production. Farms with biodigesters can process manure into biogas, reducing the amount of nitrous dioxide and methane that would otherwise enter the atmosphere. These two gases have a far greater atmospheric warming effect than does carbon dioxide (nitrous dioxide = 310 times greater, and methane = 21 times greater). Biomass is considered a sustainable energy resource because it is a product of organic processes, which naturally regenerate at a rapid cycle (as opposed to fossil fuel energy sources which take millions of years to form).

ANTHROPOCENE
The geological epoch that began when human activity started to have a significant global impact on the geochemical signatures that can be traced through ice and sediment cores. The epoch is in the process of being officially recognized, and is in common use among scientists. If approved it would either replace or immediately follow the Holocene. Used within the humanities, the term is a reference to the detrimental impact that human activity is having on the environment.

AQUAPONICS
Combining aquaculture (the raising of fish or other aquatic animals) with hydroponics (growing plants with little or no soil), aquaponics is an efficient and environmentally friendly system for food production that recycles water and requires few regular inputs. Those include: oxygen, sunlight, fish feed, water (to replace losses to evaporation and plant root uptake), and electricity (to pump, filter, and oxygenate the water). The ammonia-rich water of the aquaculture tank is cycled through biofilters where nitrifying bacteria provide nutrients to the plants downstream. After passing through the plant roots, purified water returns to the fish tank to repeat the cycle.

BIFACIAL SILICON SOLAR PANEL

Any solar panel that has solar cells on both sides. These can benefit from environments with reflected light to produce more electricity than a panel with solar cells on only one side.

BINARY (RANKINE CYCLE) GEOTHERMAL

Via the Organic Rankine Cycle (ORC), hot (but below boiling temperature) water is piped to an evaporator coil that heats a low boiling-point fluid to pressurized vapor, driving a turbine. The vapor then passes to a condenser, where cool water returns the fluid to liquid form. The Rankine cycle is named after the Scottish mechanical engineer William John Macquorn Rankine (1820–1872).

BIOFILTRATION OR BIOREMEDIATION

Living material can be used to take pollution from water, soil, or air. Through chemical processes inside plants or microorganisms, pollutants become biologically degraded or less harmful.

BIOLUMINESCENT

The emission of light by a living organism. It can be found in fireflies, glowworms, jellyfish, and many types of bacteria.

CARBON DIOXIDE (CO_2)

A naturally occurring chemical compound critical to life on Earth, carbon dioxide also functions as a greenhouse gas (GHG) in Earth's atmosphere (contributing to anthropogenic climate change and global warming). The emission of CO_2 through fossil fuel combustion by humans has, since modern industrialization, created an increase of 50% in the parts per million (ppm) concentration of the gas in Earth's atmosphere, which were at or below 280 ppm in the 18th century according to ice core data. Since 1960, its concentration has risen from 320 ppm to 420 ppm (as of 2021) and further increases threaten rapid shifts upward in global temperature and sea levels. In order to avoid a temperature rise beyond 2°C, between two-thirds and four-fifths of the known reserves of fossil fuel will need to remain unused. Increased atmospheric concentrations of CO_2 also have effects on the chemical composition of the oceans, as surface-level carbon dioxide dissolves forming other carbon compounds and leading to acidification.

CONCENTRATED SOLAR POWER (CSP)

Concentrated solar power (CSP) describes a variety of systems that use mirrors or lenses (see *heliostatic*) to concentrate the power of the sun in order to create heat energy that can then be converted into electricity.

CONVECTION LOOP

In the dynamics of fluids or gas, the tendency of higher pressure and lower pressure to equalize causes warm to migrate toward cool, thus creating a flow of gas or liquid. In closed systems with heat input in one area, a continuous loop is created as warm material flows to cool areas. See *thermosiphon heat exchanger*.

CROSS-LAMINATED TIMBER (CLT)

A composite wood panel produced by laminating multiple layers of wood in alternating grain orientation for increased strength. CLT can be fabricated from smaller and younger trees compared to dimensional lumber, which requires larger trees for conventional milling, and CLT is therefore compatible with more sustainable forest management practices.

DICHROIC FILM

Transparent film that provides a dichroic color effect—appearing to change color when viewed from different angles.

ECOTONE

The transition zone in between two biological communities.

ELECTROCHROMIC

A material that changes color or opacity when electrical voltage is applied. Smart window technology uses electrochromism, automatically tinting glass to reduce solar heat gain.

ELECTROLYSIS

Splitting water into hydrogen and oxygen.

ETHYLENE TETRAFLUOROETHYLENE (ETFE)

Ethylene tetrafluoroethylene is a fluorine-based plastic designed for high strength. It is popular as a building façade material where light transmission is desired through curved forms. Examples include the Eden Project in Cornwall, United Kingdom, and the Beijing National Aquatics Centre.

GLOSSARY (continued)

FIBONACCI SPIRAL (ALSO GOLDEN SPIRAL)

A logarithmic spiral shape that gets further from the origin each quarter turn by a factor of the golden mean. It can be approximated by tracing the corners of expanding square tiles the surface areas of which follow the Fibonacci sequence (each number is the sum of the two preceding numbers).

FOOD FOREST

Forest gardening is an ancient practice in which a variety of species of trees and plants are grown in close proximity, mimicking the biodiversity of a healthy natural forest. When practiced at large scale, the technique can also be referred to as agroforestry. Each species of plant has a unique set of roles to play in the system — some healing soils, others producing food, and others attracting a diverse population of healthy insects that reduce the risk of blight.

FREEWHEEL GENERATOR

An alternator connected to a freewheel shaft can transfer the kinetic rotational energy of the shaft into electricity. A freewheel is a spinning disc that can be engaged in one spin direction to increase its rotational energy. It is allowed to spin freely when additional external force is not applied or is applied in the opposite direction. A common illustration is a road bicycle wheel that spins faster when force is applied in the proper direction, spins as the rider coasts, and is not slowed by reverse pedaling.

FRESNEL LENS

A magnifying lens that takes the sectional geometry of a simple convex lens and flattens it by slicing it in concentric circles and shifting the annular segment profiles to create a flattened, corrugated surface. The optical effect of the lens is very similar to that of the original convex lens. The technique was perfected by Augustin-Jean Fresnel in the 1820s for application in lighthouses, and has since found practical use in a variety of optical systems including concentrator photovoltaics.

GEOFABRIC OR GEOTEXTILE

Any permeable fabric used in landscaping, construction, geotechnical engineering, or agriculture to separate, reinforce, or protect soil, or to filter or drain water within or around soils.

GRAVITY ENERGY STORAGE

Any type of energy storage system where mass is lifted in elevation to store energy and allowed to return to the lower elevation to retrieve the stored energy. Examples include pumped hydro (lifting water into a dammed reservoir), hydraulic mass (using a hydraulic lift to raise a heavy mass such as a piston in a shaft), railway (electric-drive locomotive on a track with a steep gradient), tower crane (lifting and lowering heavy block modules), and earth bucket conveyor

HELIOSTATIC (HELIOTROPIC)

The ability to follow the location of the sun in the sky and maintain an object's consistent relationship to it throughout the diurnal and seasonal shift. In solar energy technology, heliostatic mechanisms can maintain a solar cell perpendicular to the sunlight for ideal absorption and conversion, or mirrors can maintain an angle-of-incidence relationship to the sun so as to consistently reflect sunlight to a central collector.

HYBRID PHOTOVOLTAIC THERMAL (PVT)

Any system that converts solar energy into both electrical and heat energy simultaneously. Because photovoltaic panels operate at approximately 20% conversion efficiency, much of the potential solar energy is lost to heat. This heat build-up has a detrimental impact on the performance of the solar cell due to increased electrical resistance within the circuitry. PVT systems can operate at 75% total conversion efficiency (electricity + heat).

HYDROGEN FUEL CELL

A device that generates electricity by recombining hydrogen (from a canister) and oxygen (from the atmosphere). The reaction generates water and an electrical current (the opposite of electrolysis).

HYDROPHILIC

A material that is attracted to water (finds it thermodynamically favorable) and tends to become wet or dissolve in the presence of water. All hydrophilic materials are hygroscopic, but not all hygroscopic materials are hydrophilic.

HYDROPHOBIC

A material that is not attracted to water (finds it thermodynamically unfavorable). Water is repelled by (rolls cleanly off of) a hydrophobic surface.

HYGROSCOPIC

Tending to absorb moisture from the air. Examples of hygroscopic materials include cotton, wood, and sugar.

KILOWATT (kW)

Equal to 1,000 watts. See *watt*.

KILOWATT-HOUR (kWh)

Equal to 1,000 watt-hours. See *watt-hour*.

LAMELLA

A thin, translucent membrane, like the gill of a mushroom.

LED

Light-emitting diode, a semiconductor light source. An OLED is a LED that is fabricated using organic materials.

LINEAR FRESNEL REFLECTOR (LFR)

Linear Fresnel reflectors (LFR) use long, thin segments of flat mirrors to focus sunlight onto a fixed absorber located at a common focal point of the reflectors. Absorbers in LFR often contain multiple heat transfer tubes. Similar to the more common parabolic trough, this single-axis tracking concentrated reflector system heats up a transfer fluid which in turn heats water to run a steam turbine. One advantage of LFR is that the reflector mirrors are flat rather than parabolic in shape, which makes for a simpler mirror manufacturing process. See *Fresnel lens*.

LUMINESCENT SOLAR CONCENTRATOR

Using special optics, a large flat plane can create internal reflections that concentrate light hitting the surface of the plane out to the edges of the material where it is then converted into electricity with solar cells. Some versions of the technology can maintain transparency for certain wavelengths of light, while capturing others for conversion at the edge.

MEGAWATT (MW)

Equal to 1,000,000 watts. See *watt*.

MEGAWATT-HOUR (MWh)

Equal to 1,000,000 watt-hours. See *watt-hour*.

MWhe

Megawatt-hour equivalent. This unit of measurement for energy is often used when quantifying liquid fuel in comparison to electricity.

MYCELIUM

The vegetative part of a fungus, the branching threads of which are called hyphae. Mycelium can break down complex organic compounds and remediate polluted soil. When cultivated in molds, mycelium can be used to rapidly make packing materials, leather substitutes, furniture, building materials, and insulation that outperforms fiberglass, mineral wool, or polystyrene.

MYCOFILTRATION

A form of bioremediation that utilizes fungi as a means of decontaminating the environment. Fungi can be an inexpensive and efficient means of removing a wide array of pollutants (including heavy metals, hydrocarbons, pharmaceuticals, pesticides, herbicides, and other chemicals) from contaminated soils or wastewater. Byproducts of mycofiltration can make useful products, including lacasse.

MYCORRHIZAL

Having to do with the mycorrhiza, or the network of subterranean fungal colonies that merge with plant root structures. These mycorrhizal networks transmit water, carbon, nitrogen, and other nutrients and chemical information between plants, and form a critical component of a resilient and healthy forest ecosystem.

ORGANIC PHOTOVOLTAIC (OPV)

Organic PV can be manufactured in solutions that can be painted or rolled onto proper substrate materials. They have a lower conversion efficiency (13%), but can be produced at very low cost in comparison with other PV technologies because they can take advantage of roll-to-roll production techniques in which the organic photovoltaic system is "printed" onto a long, continuous sheet of substrate material.

OZONATION

A process of infusing water with ozone that is commonly used in aquaculture systems to facilitate the breakdown of organic materials.

GLOSSARY (continued)

PARABOLIC TROUGH

A type of concentrated solar power that uses a long, mirrored surface with the cross-sectional shape of a parabola. Sunlight that hits the mirror surface (at an angle parallel to the central axis of the parabola) is directed to the focal point of the parabola, thus providing energy to a heat transfer fluid that runs continuously along its length. The heated transfer fluid can be used to generate the steam required for turbine generators.

PARAMETRIC DESIGN

Any design process that incorporates mathematical algorithms to derive form. An early analog version of parametric design can be found in the structural design process of Antonio Gaudí, who used inverted force models that resulted in catenary arches, vaults, and domes. Adjusting one parameter of the model results in downstream changes to other components. Parametric techniques allow designers to mirror complex organic and natural forms and to rapidly iterate variations.

PERMACULTURE

Adapting the cycles observed within healthy natural ecosystems to agricultural practices, thereby maintaining healthy soil, enhancing ecosystem services, improving resilience, and diversifying crop yields, while eliminating the use of pesticides and herbicides. Permaculture often incorporates Indigenous knowledge and traditions, as well as regenerative agricultural practices that draw atmospheric carbon into soil (biosequestration).

PHOTOVOLTAIC (PV)

The photovoltaic effect, first recognized by A. E. Becquerel in 1839, is the ability of a material to produce direct current electricity when exposed to solar radiation. Silicon (Si) is a semiconductor material that displays the photovoltaic effect. It was the first material to be employed in solar cells and is still the most prevalent. It can be applied for use in either a crystalline (wafer) form, or in a noncrystalline (amorphous) form. There are two types of crystalline silicon: monocrystalline and polycrystalline (aka multicrystalline). Monocrystalline is expensive to manufacture (because it requires cutting slices from cylindrical ingots of silicon crystals that are grown with the Czochralski process) but it displays a high conversion efficiency (around 23%). Polycrystalline is easier to manufacture than monocrystalline silicon and is more versatile, but has lower conversion (around 18%).

PHOTOVOLTAIC THERMAL (PVT)

Any system that converts solar energy into both electrical and heat energy simultaneously. Because photovoltaic panels operate at approximately 20% conversion efficiency, much of the potential solar energy is lost to heat. This heat build-up has a detrimental impact on the performance of the solar cell due to increased electrical resistance within the circuitry. PVT systems can operate at 75% total conversion efficiency (electricity + heat).

PHYTODEPURATION

An engineered system that reproduces the natural water purification processes of a wetland environment. The artificial basins are typically filled with soil and aquatic plants that can be floating, flooded, or emerging. Phytodepuration is a natural way to filter and treat wastewater through nutrient and chemical interactions between soil, bacteria, and plants.

PHYTOREMEDIATION

Using plants to clean up polluted soil, water, and air.

PIEZOELECTRIC GENERATOR

A device that generates electrical power from pressure force. Common application of a piezoelectric device is as the ignition source for gas range and grill "push starters." Piezoelectric discs or torriods can be stacked within a flexible pole to generate electrical current from the bending of the pole (piezoelectric stacked actuators).

POLYCULTURE

A type of agricultural practice where multiple species are grown together, imitating the diversity of natural ecosystems. Common industrial farming tends to grow crops as monocultures, depleting soils and limiting biodiversity, which can lead to increased pest infestation.

PYROLYSIS

A thermochemical decomposition process that differs from anaerobic digestion or fermentation, requiring very little water, and using biomass feedstock to produce solid biochar, along with bio-oils, which resemble light crude oil, and syngas. Flash pyrolysis, in which feedstock is heated quickly for two seconds to between 350°C and 500°C, is the most efficient method. The heat energy can be supplied by concentrated solar power technology to maintain carbon neutrality. Biochar can help sequester carbon from the atmosphere when used as a fertilizer in soils. When combusted for heat, biochar solids burn cleaner and put off more consistent heat than wood.

REGENERATE

To defy entropy through the maintenance of systems that cycle and recycle energy. Employ systems that produce resources to support human thriving and biodiversity. To leverage the power of the sun, human energy, and rapidly renewable resources to give back more than is input or invested into the system — generating resources such as energy, biomass, or clean water, or generating new investments into social systems.

REVERSE OSMOSIS

A process for the purification of water using semi-permeable membranes that separate ions and particles. Artificial pressure is applied using a pump to overcome osmotic pressure and leave impurities on the pressurized side of the membrane, while pure water is collected on the unpressurized side.

SCHREBERGARTEN

A Schrebergarten also known as a kleingarten (small garden), is a plot of public land — usually around 400 square meters — maintained by a private individual or family. Located on the city's peripheries, they are overseen by local cooperative associations and clubs. These organizations have their own regulations and restrictions on the use of the gardens. Some place restrictions on the size of various garden elements, such as the garden house, area for vegetables, flowers, and greenhouse. Kleingarten plots are not allowed to be used as a residential space or mail address. Small ponds or pools are allowed under certain safety regulations, similar to the American HOA (homeowners association). Some are very strict, while others are open for expression and creativity. The plural is Schrebergärten or kleingärten.

SOLAR DISTILLATION FOR DESALINATION (SOLAR STILL)

The solar humidification-dehumidification method (HDH) is a thermal water desalination technique based on evaporation of saltwater and condensation of the humid air that results. The process is very similar to the natural water cycle, but accelerated by the greenhouse effect of the enclosure.

SOLAR THERMAL

Solar radiation used to heat a medium such as water or air.

SOLAR UPDRAFT (SOLAR CHIMNEY)

Combines the chimney/stack effect and greenhouse effect with wind turbines located at the base of a tall tower. The tower is surrounded by a greenhouse which serves to create superheated air at the ground level. With a sufficiently tall chimney structure, the air temperature at the top of the tower will be cool enough to provide pressure differential convection movement of air through the turbines.

SORBENT

Any solid material that attracts and absorbs (holds within) or adsorbs (holds on the surface) a different liquid or gas material.

STIRLING HEAT ENGINE

Device that converts heat into mechanical energy with high efficiency. This mechanical energy can then be used to power an electrical generator.

SWALE

A shallow channel with gently sloping sides designed to manage water runoff, filter pollutants, and increase rainwater infiltration. Bioswales are planted with hearty local species that provide additional water filtration and stormwater attenuation.

THERMOELECTRIC GENERATOR (TEG), ALSO KNOWN AS SEEBACK GENERATOR

In 1821 Thomas Johann Seebeck discovered that different metals respond uniquely to temperature differences to create a magnetic field. Modern thermoelectric generators that make use of this physical property of metals (their Seebeck coefficient) are able to generate a voltage when the "hot side" is exposed to heat and the "cold side" is sufficiently insulated to maintain a differential temperature.

THERMOSIPHON HEAT EXCHANGER

A system wherein heat is circulated passively using natural convection and without the need for an mechanical pump. See *convection loop*.

THIN-FILM

As applied to photovoltaics, any of a variety of non-crystalline solar cell technologies that can be applied in very thin layers, thus reducing material costs. Sometimes referred to as *second-generation photovoltaic cells*.

GLOSSARY (continued)

TURBINE ROTOR

The moving part of a turbine engine which consists of a drum or a shaft with blades attached to it.

TRIBOELECTRIC EFFECT

The triboelectric effect describes the production of electrical charge when a material of one kind is placed in frictional contact with a material of a different kind. Commonly referred to as "static electricity" the effect can be seen when drawing a plastic comb through hair, or moving a rubber balloon against a shaggy carpet.

TRIBOELECTRIC NANOGENERATORS (TENG)

Triboelectric nanogenerators (TENG) are a relatively new kind of energy harvesting technology developed by Professor Zhong Lin Wang and his team at Georgia Institute of Technology in 2012. It uses the triboelectric effect combined with electrostatic induction. Since then, many universities have been working on increasing the energy density and productivity of TENG. The technology has the potential to generate between 50 and 300 watts per square meter by harnessing the kinetic energy of wind, waves, or the movement of people. Triboelectric nanogenerators produce electricity by taking advantage of the electrostatic properties of different materials. Kinetic energy moves the two different materials together and apart and this movement sends a flow of electrons that can be distributed for use, or stored in a battery.

UTILITY-SCALE

Significant enough power generation so as to warrant the distribution of the energy to the utility grid (as opposed to on-site power generation for local use).

VERTICAL AXIS WIND TURBINE

Any wind turbine in which the rotational axis is vertical in orientation (perpendicular to the ground plane). Types of vertical axis wind turbines include Savonius, Darrieus (eggbeater), and Giromills.

VORTEX BLADELESS WIND TURBINE

A wind energy conversion device that does not require rotating blades or other moving parts. It instead makes use of resonance within a system that is vibrated by the force of wind across the body of the device.

WATT (W)

Unit of measure of electrical power equivalent to 1/746 horsepower. W = Volts × Amperes

WATT-HOUR

A measure of electrical energy equivalent to one watt of power used or produced for a one-hour duration.

WIND MICROTURBINE

A small wind turbine with less than 3,000 watt peak capacity. Pico wind turbines are even smaller with peak capacity of ess than 500 watts.

WIND TURBINE

A rotary engine driven by the force of passing wind that can convert rotational force into electrical power.

INDEX

220	A Celebration of Light, Water, and Mirror	104	GIRASOLI	200	Spinelli Pillar
112	Artee	86	H.E.A.R.T.	202	Square Roots
116	BAU(M): The Fractal Tree	170	Hyperbolic Garden	204	Tetravoltaics: Modular Tetrahedron Framework for Energy and Food Production
64	Bloom	60	HyperSquares		
120	Bloom: Energy Infrastructure as an Ecosystem Catalyst in a Dry Land	190	In Time?		
		96	Island of Nature and Art	144	The Barracks: Spinelli Ecological Intersection
		56	Kaleidoscopic Dune		
214	Bloom: Purpose of Nature	192	Knitted Orchards	179	The Dovecote & The Fallen Dovecote
186	Butterfly	152	ma duneland	208	The Energy+Art Garden
188	Corridor of Life	194	Mannheim Murmurations	148	The Flourishing Nest
166	Cropergy: Essential Source of Life	156	Modular Innovation Cube	212	The Solar Poplars
		210	MOUND	182	The Solar Root
74	Current Notations	82	Offline Park	221	The Sun Flower
132	Der Bienenstock (The Hive)	68	Plane of Water	184	The Wave
		207	Planktonic Synergy	162	treEcoTopia
222	Eco-Art Pollinators	196	Poop, Play, Power	108	Trees and Seesaws
124	Energiebaum	158	Post-Terra	100	Unfold
50	Energy Circus	176	Power Nebh	213	Vibranergy: Energy Turned Into Vibrancy
128	Energy Generation	178	Power Walk		
78	eTREE, an Homage to Nature	198	Room to Breathe	216	Walking in the Fields of Gold
		136	Sky Wings		
211	Flower Farm	180	Solar Leaf	218	Windwald
215	Flower Garden	140	Speak Up	90	Yggdrasil
206	Flower Power: Forever in Bloom				

ACKNOWLEDGMENTS

It was an honor and privilege to work in the City of Mannheim over the past few years. We were welcomed warmly by everyone and loved Baden-Württemberg from the start. So much care has been taken with the design of the cities, parks, and greenways of the region. This level of consideration for the public realm can certainly be found in the masterplanning of BUGA 23, Spinelli Park, and the Climate Corridor. We look forward to continuing to watch the progress as the park evolves into its full splendor with the hope that one or more of the ideas contained in this book might be implemented for the benefit of the city.

We are especially thankful to the German Bundesgartenschau for inviting LAGI to Mannheim. The entire BUGA 23 team is a delight to collaborate with and it has been a pleasure getting to know them over the past few years. Thank you Michael Schnellbach, Kirsten Batzler, Anna Maier, Andrea Bergbold, Corinna Brod, Rebecca Grunert, Lina Mayer, Hanspeter Faas, and everyone who has worked so hard to make BUGA 23 a success.

Thanks to the City of Mannheim and to Lord Mayor Dr. Peter Kurz for embracing the idea of bringing together renewable energy and art in public space to help advance public desire for climate solutions.

Thanks to the shortlisting committee who spent the better part of a sunny Saturday in October getting to know the submissions to LAGI 2022 and arriving at the shortlist that were presented to the final jury. And thanks to the expert jurors who gave their valuable time to learn about the shortlisted projects and put together their rankings. You'll find their names listed on the following pages.

Special thanks goes out to Tina Nailor, who was seemingly sent to us from heaven to help manage LAGI 2022. Tina's local knowledge and background in urban planning proved indispensable and she kept everything running smoothly.

Thank you to all of the artists, engineers, architects, landscape architects, builders, makers, inventors, and dreamers who participated in LAGI 2022 Mannheim. We hope your beautiful ideas will soon come to life and that you will continue to integrate renewable energy and regenerative systems into every project.

Thanks to Ann Rosenthal, who poured through every word, letter, and comma to get this book as close to perfect as possible, and to Paul Schifino, whose incredible eye and design sensibility have made this book so beautiful and readable. Paul is a member of our Board of Directors. We would also like to thank him in that capacity along with fellow Board members Todd Bartholl, Christopher Choa, Deborah Hosking, Martin Pasqualetti, Victor Pérez-Rul, Tim Mollette-Parks, and George Riley Thomas II.

Thanks to Tunnel Monster Collective for their fantastic game design collaboration that resulted in *Kleingarten*, the educational component of LAGI 2022 Mannheim.

Thank you to all of the great people who we had the pleasure of meeting during our time in Mannheim.

And thank you to the incredible team at HIRMER. We are so grateful that the creators behind the LAGI designs have their work seen so widely.

This book is dedicated to all those who have suffered dark, freezing nights without access to energy during this most recent energy crisis. We hope to see the day when people are no longer subjected to the failures of infrastructure that follow from reliance on the volatile and fragile energy systems that dominate our present global petroculture.

Offline Park
David Vardy, Jiayi Xu, Yuzhang Su, Jinyu Li, Xuanrun Yi, Evan Saarinen

See page 82

LAGI 2022 Mannheim Jurors

Klaus Gasteiger
Social Engagement Site
Ludwigshafen, BASF SE

Andreas Kipar
Landscape Architect,
Co-Founder, CEO, and Creative
Director LAND

Dr. Peter Kurz
Lord Mayor of Mannheim

Dr. Clark Miller
Professor; Director, Center for
Energy & Society, School for the
Future of Innovation in Society,
Arizona State University

Dr. Heinz Ossenbrink
Former European Commission
Joint Research Centre

Michael Schnellbach
CEO, BUGA 23

Dr. Alessandra Scognamiglio
Architect, Senior Researcher
at the National Agency for
New Technologies, Energy
and Sustainable Economic
Development (ENEA)

Asha Singhal
Regenerative Designer,
Hybrid Futures

Peter Slavenburg
Co-founder, NorthernLight

Helen Turner
Artistic Director and Chief
Curator, E-WERK Luckenwalde

Marjan van Aubel
Solar Designer

LAGI 2022 Mannheim Shortlist Committee

Dr. Amadeus Bach

Kirsten Batzler

Elena Berberich

Andrea Bergbold

Susann El Salamoni

Dennis Ewert

Christian Franke

Rhea Häni

Marc Hunger

Alexandra Kriegel

Birgit Lang

David Linse

Anna Maier

Thomas Neumann

Christiane Ram

Miriam Rausch

Tjark Siefkes

Mireille Solomon

Artee

Jonathan Hernandez, Lorenz Riedel, Nawapan Suntorachai, Maria Matheou, Felipe Romero

See page 112

© Land Art Generator Initiative, Pittsburgh (PA), and Hirmer, 2023

All text © the authors or their estates unless otherwise noted. All works © the artists, artist teams, or their estates unless otherwise noted. All project descriptions © the artists, artist teams, or their estates unless otherwise noted.

Cover: *Plane of Water*, Zsuzsa Péter

Published by:
Hirmer Verlag
Bayerstraße 57-59
80335 München Germany
www.hirmerverlag.de

Editorial direction: Robert Ferry, Elizabeth Monoian
Project management Hirmer Publishers: Rainer Arnold
Senior editor Hirmer Publishers: Elisabeth Rochau-Shalem
Copy editing and proof reading: Ann Rosenthal
Design: Paul Schifino, schifinodesign.com
Pre-press: Reproline Mediateam, Unterföhring, Germany
Printing and binding: Printer Trent s.r.l.
Printed in Italy

Library of Congress Control Number: 2023901532
Bibliographic information published by the Deutsche Nationalbibliothek The Deutsche Nationalbibliothek lists this publication in the Deutsche Nationalbibliografie; detailed bibliographic data is available on the Internet at http://www.dnb.de.

ISBN 978-3-7774-4093-4

LAGI 2022 Mannheim was held in partnership with BUGA 23.

The Land Art Generator Initiative is a US-based non-profit organization.
www.landartgenerator.org

Bloom
**Mateusz Góra,
Agata Gryszkiewicz**
See page 64